CREATIVE FOOD PROCESSOR COOKING

Ethel Lang Graham

WEATHERVANE
BOOKS

We would like to thank the following companies for
supplying us with information and photographs of their
food processors:
Cuisinarts, Inc.
Braun North America
Farberware (Division of L.C.A. Corp.)
Jack Levin and Associates, Inc.
Kitchen Aid Division - Hobart Manufacturing Co.
Magic Mill International
Oster Corporation
Robot Coupe, U.S.A.
Sunbeam Corporation
Varco, Inc.
Vita Mix Corporation

Contents

introduction to the cuisinart food processor

The Cuisinart food processor is unique among all types of food processors that blend, mix, shred, and slice. Because of its large, flat, S-shaped, serrated stainless-steel blade, this machine will chop meats and nuts, as well as ingredients for main dishes, soups, and sandwich fillings. Carefully control its running time or turn the motor on and off quickly to reduce the speed of the blades, and it will chop coarsely and uniformly. Allow it to run, and it will mince or puree so finely that it can actually be used to make peanut butter.

But that's not all! The powerful blade is large enough to mix batters for quick breads, knead dough for a $4\frac{1}{2} \times 8\frac{1}{2}$-inch loaf, prepare pasta dough, blend crepe batter in seconds, mash potatoes, and prepare cookies with chopped nuts in a few brief steps. It will make mayonnaise, spreads, herb butters, dips, and pie crusts and be altogether a pleasure to own and operate.

The Cuisinart food processor comes equipped with several very easy-to-store attachments. The slicing disk rapidly slices any foods trimmed to fit the tube, with no danger to your fingers. The shredding disk grates or shreds cheeses and vegetables in a whiz. A plastic blade, similar in shape to the metal blade, is used for mixing meat salads and spreads when no further chopping is desired.

The machine is not only a joy to use, it takes up less than a square foot of counter space and is conveniently stored. You will surely never put away such an attractive piece of equipment. Its base surface is easy to wipe clean, and the cord is smooth and crease-free, so it does not accumulate the usual kitchen grease and dust. All parts, except the pusher, can be washed safely in a dishwasher.

The many safety features are well designed for your protection. The on–off switch is on the lid, and the processor will not operate unless the lid is in place. The pusher and tube protect the fingers.

In this book I have tried to keep recipes simple, combining steps where possible, and to limit calories wherever it was practical. Should you want more calories in any recipe, they certainly are easy to add. Often two choices are given: milk or cream, yogurt or sour cream, sour cream or mayonnaise. The first in each pair is lower in calories. While butter and margarine are identical in caloric value, butter has a better flavor but contains cholesterol; margarine contains none.

If you have never made bread, try making it with this machine. I highly recommend the whole-grain recipes. Try the pasta and the good sauces, the herb butters as spreads or accompaniments to meats and vegetables, the spicy Mexican dishes, and the fondue dips.

Recipes in this book were developed and tested with the Cuisinart food processor, Model CFP 5. Similar styles of food processors are now being manufactured by other companies and may be used to prepare most of the goodies featured here. However, some machines are not as powerful. Some are driven by a belt rather than a drive shaft and may stall quickly in bread dough. Check with your local kitchen specialty store where several brands and models of processors are demonstrated. They can give you the latest information on prices, models, and operation, as well as availability of service, parts, and optional attachments. You may be willing to sacrifice power or features for a less expensive machine.

precautions and tips for use

1) The pusher was designed for the tube. Use it. Never put your fingers down the tube while slicing or shredding.
2) Do not remove the lid until the disks have stopped spinning, or food will spin off the blade and fly all over you and the cooking area.
3) If you have not followed instruction number 2, above, never use your hands to stop a spinning disk. The edges are sharp!
4) The metal blade is sharp and heavy. Handle it with care lest it drop on your foot.
5) Do not put the pusher in the dishwasher or it will develop a leak at the top seam. (This can be resealed with silicone tub sealer — words of the experienced.) Blades, disks, spatula, and lexan bowl and lid are dishwasher safe.
6) Process only 2½ cups of liquid ingredients in the bowl at one time or the liquid will seep slowly out of the bowl from the center hole for the drive shaft. Should this happen, no harm is done. Whisk it off the easily cleaned base with a dishcloth.
7) Do not try to grate hard cheeses, Parmesan or Romano, with the shredding disk. This may damage the drive shaft and disk.
8) You must use a serrated disk to slice pepperoni. If you have a machine with a smooth slicing disk, do not attempt pepperoni.
9) The metal blade will whip non-dairy toppings or whipping cream satisfactorily, but, for greater aeration and volume, use a mixer. The blade will not whip air into egg whites; use a mixer. It will do a satisfactory job of creaming a butter–egg–sugar mixture, however.
10) To grind raw meat, cut it into 1-inch cubes and process it one cup at a time with the metal blade. Do not overprocess.
11) To slice vegetables crosswise, wedge several in the tube so the pieces stand upright.
12) Vegetables may be sliced lengthwise if they are trimmed to fit lengthwise into the tube and are stacked.
13) Try to keep children from licking the luscious batters from the sharp metal blade. Maybe they'll be satisfied with the spatula and bowl.
14) Avoid damage to the spring in the start mechanism by storing the lid on the bowl in the "motor-off" position.
15) Read the machine's instruction booklet thoroughly.

Cuisinart Food Processor CFP-5
Retail Price $225.00

The Cuisinart Food Processor will chop, knead, shred, blend, and slice. It is handsomely designed and takes up less room than the average toaster. Included with the machine are a stainless steel serrated slicing disk, a shredding disk, a chopping blade, and a plastic mixing blade. Optional parts include a smooth slicing disk for vegetables, a ripple-cut fine-slicing disk for vegetables, a fine-shredding disk, a French-fry disk, a julienne disk, and a juice-extractor.

OTHER FOOD PROCESSORS

Many types of food processors are currently available. Their prices and the tasks they perform vary widely. Some are used exclusively for slicing and grating, others for mixing and blending, while some have numerous attachments to handle widely assorted tasks.

Recipes in this book were developed for and tested with the Cuisinart Food Processor, model CFP-5. Information on other food processors is presented here for your information. Many kitchen specialty stores demonstrate these machines. Be sure to check with these sources for prices and up-to-date information on consumer satisfaction and operation.

Bosch Magic Mixer
Retail Price $239.50

The Bosch Standard Kitchen Machine comes equipped with a plastic bowl (4½-quart capacity), wire beaters, dough hook, and a blender (6-cup capacity). Optional attachments include a slicer/shredder, juicer, citrus/lemon-squeezer, an ice cream freezer, a coffee/nut-grinder, an extrusion shredder, a meat/food-grinder, pastry press, manual handle for use without electrical power, grater, noodle/pasta attachment, sausage-maker, berry press, and a grain mill with grinding stones.

Braun Kitchen Machine KM-321
Retail Price $160.00

The attractive Braun Kitchen Machine possesses a 400-watt heavy-duty motor with 3 speeds. The basic unit comes equipped with a large mixing bowl. The powerful machine readily kneads bread. Optional attachments include a coffee- and nut-grinder, a citrus-juicer, a meat-grinder, a shredder/slicer with 5 cutters, and a blender with a 4-cup capacity. All attachments are assembled or removed without tools and screws.

Epicurean Food Processor
Retail Price $99.99

The Epicurean Food Processor is equipped with a grating disk, a shredding disk, a slicing blade, and a plastic mixing blade. The base is compact and takes up little counter space. All parts are dishwasher-safe. The motor is made by General Electric.

Kitchen Aid K45

The Kitchen Aid K45 has a 4½-quart stainless bowl and a 250-watt motor. A flat beater, wire whip, and a dough hook are standard equipment with the machine. Available attachments include a can-opener, a grain mill, a food-grinder, a slicer/shredder with 4 cones, a juice-extractor, and a colander and sieve.

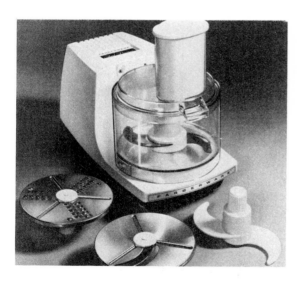

Farberware Food Processor No. 286
Retail Price $120.00

The Farberware Food Processor comes equipped with a see-through bowl and cover. The base is high-strength aluminum colored a light beige. The base is easy to clean with a damp cloth; all other parts are dishwasher-safe. Standard attachments include a chopping blade, shredding blade, slicing blade, and a plastic mixing blade.

Oster Kitchen Center FoodCrafter
Retail Price $134.95

The Oster Kitchen Center FoodCrafter is actually 4 appliances in one unit. It features a heavy-duty blender with a 5-cup capacity, a grinder head with 2 cutting disks, a mixer arm, 4-quart and 1½-quart glass bowls, and a FoodCrafter slicer/shredder/salad-maker with 3 cutting disks. Optional accessories include a doughmaker arm, a citrus-juicer, a can-opener, an ice-crusher, a cutting board designed to sit over the base, and a sausage-making kit. This versatile processor is available in gold, white, or avocado.

Robot Vertical Cutter R-2
Retail Price $399.00

The Robot Model R-2 Vertical Cutter is equipped with a 2½-quart cutter bowl and a side discharge attachment for continuous feeding. Standard attachments include a chopping blade and your choice of 2 slicer/grater disks. Optional attachments include many assorted slicer and grater disks and a juicer attachment.

Varco Salad Maker and Meat Grinder
Retail Price about $40.00

The Varco Salad Maker and Meat Grinder is compact and easy to store. The salad-maker head has 4 interchangeable rust-resistant cones for grating, shredding, and slicing. The meat-grinder has 2 tempered-steel cutting blades for grinding raw or cooked meat.

Sunbeam Deluxe Mixmaster
Retail Price $100.00

The Sunbeam Deluxe Mixmaster Mixer is available in three colors and chrome. It has a 12-speed dial, dough hooks, beaters, and 4-quart and 1½-quart mixing bowls. The mixer head can be removed from the stand for portable use.

Optional accessories include a juicer, meat-grinder/food-chopper, and stainless steel bowls.

Vita Mix 3600
Retail Price $200.00

The Vita Mix 3600 mixes, grinds, grates, purees, and liquifies. It has a pressurized serving spigot for serving juices and soups. The blades can be reversed almost instantly to eliminate clogging. When the machine is run on its highest speed, it will cook or heat foods with the heat generated by friction of the blades against the food. No accessory parts are needed.

appetizers

surprise cheese puffs

Prepare these in advance and heat just before serving.

Yield: About 24

> **4 ounces sharp cheddar cheese,
>   shredded with the shredding
>   disk**
> **¼ cup cold butter, cut into 4 pieces**
> **½ cup sifted all-purpose flour**
> **¼ teaspoon salt**
> **½ teaspoon paprika**
> **24 olives, or cocktail onions, or
>   cubes of cooked ham, etc.**

Place shredded cheese, butter, flour, salt, and paprika in processor bowl. Process with metal blade until smooth.

Form a teaspoonful of the mixture around each olive, onion, or piece of ham. Place on an ungreased baking sheet and refrigerate.

Just before serving, bake in a 400°F oven for 10 to 15 minutes or until golden.

champagne–fruit cocktail

Yield: 6 servings

> **⅔ cup fresh pineapple, cut into
>   1-inch cubes**
> **1 peeled orange, sliced, seeds
>   removed**
> **⅔ cup fresh strawberries**
> **3 tablespoons sugar**
> **1 bottle champagne, chilled**

Place fruit and sugar in processor bowl and process with metal blade until finely chopped.

Place some of the mixture in each of 6 chilled champagne glasses. Fill with champagne and serve at once.

cocktail cream puffs with sour cream and caviar

cocktail cream puffs with sour cream and caviar

Yield: 24

**2 dozen small Cream Puff Shells
    (see Index)**
½ pint sour cream
2 (or more) tablespoons caviar

Prepare small Cream Puff Shells as recipe directs. Cut off tops.

Combine sour cream and caviar. Fill shells. Replace tops. Serve at once.

Cream puffs may also be filled with many of the Sandwich Spreads (see Index) and used as appetizers.

olive–nut hors d'oeuvres

Use small olives, if you wish, and you can make more.

Yield: 8 hors d'oeuvres

**3 ounces cream cheese, cut into 4
    pieces**
¼ cup almonds
1 teaspoon milk
8 large stuffed olives, patted dry
Paprika (optional)

Place cheese, almonds, and milk in processor bowl and process with metal blade until almonds are minced.

Form mixture around each of the 8 olives. Chill. Serve on toothpicks.

These can be rolled in paprika, more chopped almonds, or parsley chopped with the metal blade, for added color and interest.

ingredients for steak tartare

steak tartare

Yield: About 2 cups

½ pound fresh beef, cut into
  1-inch cubes
1 teaspoon Worcestershire
  sauce
2 teaspoons cognac
1 egg yolk
Dash Tabasco sauce
½ teaspoon paprika
Salt and pepper to
  taste

garnishes

Olives
Cocktail onions
Anchovy fillets with capers
Sliced gherkins
Onion, chopped finely with the
  metal blade
Crackers or thin slices of dark rye
  or pumpernickel snack
  bread

Place beef, Worcestershire sauce, cognac, egg yolk, Tabasco sauce, and paprika in processor bowl. Process with metal blade until beef is finely chopped. Place mixture in a bowl set in cracked ice. Place garnishes in small bowls. Guests spread meat on crackers or bread and top with a garnish.

mushroom cocktail

Like seasoned raw mushrooms? Try this!

Yield: 4 to 6 servings

½ pound fresh mushrooms
2 tablespoons vinegar
1 teaspoon horseradish
¾ cup catsup
Lettuce cups

Wedge mushrooms sideways in the tube and slice into "T" shapes with the slicing disk.

Combine vinegar, horseradish, and catsup. Add mushrooms. Chill and serve in lettuce cups with crackers.

cocktail meatballs in beer sauce

Yield: 20 to 30

1½ pounds lean beef, cut into
**   1-inch cubes**
2 teaspoons salt
½ teaspoon pepper
Vegetable oil for browning

½ cup beer
½ cup chili sauce
1 teaspoon soy sauce
1 teaspoon sugar

Process the beef with the metal blade, one cup at a time, until finely chopped. Season with salt and pepper and form into firm 1-inch balls. Brown in oil in a skillet. Place in a chafing dish or fondue pot with remaining ingredients. Heat.

Guests serve themselves directly from the chafing dish with toothpicks.

shrimp or scallop cocktail

Yield of sauce: About 1 cup

Chilled, cooked shrimps or scallops
Lettuce

cocktail sauce

¼ cup catsup
⅓ cup lemon juice
½ teaspoon Worcestershire sauce
1 teaspoon salt

1 tablespoon prepared horseradish
1 small stalk celery, minced with
**   the metal blade**

Arrange shrimps over lettuce in cocktail glasses. Combine sauce ingredients and serve over shrimps.

camembert spread

Yield: About 1¼ cups

spread

   ⅓ cup cold butter, cut into 4
       pieces
   8 ounces Camembert cheese
   1 teaspoon paprika
   1 small onion
   8 blades of chives, cut into 1-inch
       pieces

garnish

   Small pretzels
   Circle of pumpernickel bread
   Radish rose

camembert spread

Place ingredients for spread in processor bowl and process with metal blade until onions are minced. Arrange on a plate and garnish with pretzels. Place bread circle in center and top with the radish as pictured. Serve with crackers or thinly sliced dark bread.

herring in sour cream

The food processor makes perfectly thin onion slices, so desirable in this good appetizer.

Yield: 2 cups

   2 6-ounce cans herring fillets
   1 medium onion, sliced with the
       slicing disk
  24 whole black peppercorns
   2 crushed bay leaves
   1 cup sour cream
   3 tablespoons sauterne

Cut fillets into bite-size pieces. Combine in a bowl with onion, pepper, and bay leaves.

Mix sour cream and wine and stir into fillet mixture. Cover and refrigerate 4 to 8 hours before serving. Keeps for 1 or 2 days.

dips and chips

Dips for chips, crackers, vegetables, wedges of Pita Bread (see Index) are easily prepared in your food processor. A smooth base is usually formed by processing cream cheese, grated cheese, sour cream, or other ingredients with the metal blade. Ingredients that are to remain coarsely chopped in the base mixture are added. The metal blade is turned on and off quickly several times to reduce the speed of the blades and to produce a uniform, coarse chopping of these ingredients, rather than mincing.

Can you imagine making assorted chips in your processor? Try them — see how fresh they taste. Be sure to use fresh oil for frying!

Many of the dips included here can be used with vegetable dippers. Cut vegetables by hand so the slices or pieces are firm enough to scoop up the dip. Serve them in small glass flowerpots with the dip in a large bowl or larger glass flowerpot.

suggestions for vegetable dippers

Carrot sticks
Cauliflower florets on toothpicks
Celery sticks, crisped in ice water
Unpeeled cucumber slices or sticks, crisped in ice water
French-fried potatoes
Fresh green beans, tips removed
Green pepper rings or wedges
Scallions
Fresh snow pea pods, tips and strings removed
Unpeeled summer squash slices
Fresh turnip sticks
Unpeeled zucchini slices

other dippers

Fresh fruit, lightly brushed with pineapple juice to prevent browning
Cooked shrimps on toothpicks

banana chips

Yield: 1 or more cups chips

Vegetable oil for frying
2 to 3 green bananas
Salt

Heat oil in a deep pan to 390°F. Peel and slice the bananas crosswise with the slicing disk. Fry the slices a few at a time until light brown, 1 to 2 minutes. Remove from fat and drain on paper towels. Sprinkle with salt while still warm.

pumpkin chips

Yield: Varies with amount of pumpkin used

Fresh pumpkin, seeded, pared, and cut into 2 × 4-inch sections

Vegetable oil for frying
Salt or garlic salt

Slice the pumpkin sections with the slicing disk. Soak slices in water for 1 hour. Remove and pat dry. Fry in oil at 360°F, a few slices at a time, for about 2 minutes or until lightly browned. Drain on paper towels. Sprinkle with salt or garlic salt or a mixture of salt, ginger, and nutmeg. A mixture of garlic salt and curry powder is also good.

corn chips

Yield: Varies with the number of tortillas used

6 to 12 Tortillas (see Contents)
Vegetable oil for frying
Salt or garlic salt

Prepare tortillas according to directions given elsewhere in this book. After heating, cut them into wedges with a knife or pizza cutter. Let dry at room temperature overnight.

Heat oil to 375° F and drop in several chips at a time. Fry until lightly browned, 1 or 2 minutes. Drain on paper towels. Sprinkle with salt while still warm.

potato chips

With a food processor, homemade potato chips are easily prepared. The potatoes can be sliced uniformly and thinly enough for professional looking chips that you know are fresh and tasty.

Yield: Varies with the number of potatoes used

Fresh potatoes, peeled, and
**   trimmed to fit the processor tube**
Vegetable oil for frying
Salt

Slice the potatoes with the slicing disk. Rinse slices in cold water to remove excess surface starch. Drain and pat dry. Fry a few slices at a time in oil at 375° F until very lightly browned. Drain on paper towels. Sprinkle with salt while still warm.

cucumber green goddess dip

Yield: 1⅓ cups

2 3-ounce packages cream cheese,
**   each cut into 4 pieces**
2 slices onion
½ teaspoon salt
¼ teaspoon cumin or oregano
½ unpeeled cucumber, cut into 6
**   pieces**

Place cream cheese, onion, salt, and cumin in processor bowl. Process with metal blade until smooth, about 15 seconds. Add cucumber, and process by turning on and off quickly until cucumber is minced. Serve chilled with chips or vegetable dippers.

16

pink ham dip

Yield: 1¾ cups

    1 8-ounce package cream cheese
    ½ cup mayonnaise
    2 tablespoons catsup
    1 3-inch stalk celery
    2 ounces cooked ham, cut into 3
        pieces
    2 tablespoons fresh parsley leaves
    Salt if necessary
    8 to 10 small olives

Place all ingredients except olives in the food processor bowl and process with the metal blade until smooth, about 15 seconds. Add olives and process until finely chopped. Serve chilled with crackers or vegetable dippers.

guacamole dip

Yield: 1 cup

    1 ripe avocado, peeled and pitted
    ¼ onion
    1 teaspoon lemon juice
    ½ teaspoon salt
    ⅛ teaspoon freshly ground black
        pepper
    ¼ teaspoon ascorbic or citrus acid
        mixture (optional)

Place all ingredients in food processor bowl and process with metal blade until smooth, about 15 seconds. Serve at once with chips or vegetable dippers.

Dip darkens quickly and cannot be stored. To delay darkening, ¼ teaspoon ascorbic or citric acid mixture may be added during processing.

fish dip

Use fish in season flounder, mackerel, cod, etc.

Yield: 2 cups

    1 cup sour cream
    1 3-ounce package cream cheese,
        cut into 4 pieces
    1 scallion, cut into 1-inch pieces
    1 tablespoon horseradish
    ½ teaspoon salt
    8 ounces cooked fish
    2 hard-cooked eggs, quartered

Place first five ingredients in processor bowl. Process with metal blade until cheese is blended and scallion is minced, about 15 seconds. Add fish and eggs. Process by turning on and off quickly 4 or 5 times, until fish and eggs are finely chopped. Serve cold with chips or vegetable dippers.

clam dip

Yield: 1½ cups

1 8-ounce package cream cheese, cut into 8 pieces
1 2-inch piece scallion

1 teaspoon Worcestershire sauce
2 8-ounce cans minced clams, drained

Process the cream cheese, scallion, and Worcestershire sauce with the metal blade until the scallion is minced, about 15 seconds. Add clams and process by turning blade on and off quickly 2 or 3 times to blend. Serve chilled with crackers, chips, or vegetable dippers.

gail's spinach dip

A good conversation-starter at parties.

Yield: 1 cup

3 scallions, cut into 1-inch pieces
2 cups mayonnaise
1 10-ounce package frozen spinach, thawed, lightly drained, large stems removed
Garlic salt and pepper to taste

Place scallions and mayonnaise in processor bowl. Process with metal blade until scallions are minced. Add spinach, and process by turning blade on and off quickly to blend. Season to taste with garlic salt and pepper. Chill and serve with vegetable dippers.

baked-bean and ham dip

Yield: 1½ cups

1-pound can baked beans in molasses sauce
3 ounces cooked ham, cut into 5 pieces
1½ tablespoons horseradish
1 tablespoon Worcestershire sauce
½ medium onion, cut into 4 pieces
1 or 2 drops Tabasco sauce

Place all ingredients in the food processor bowl and process with the metal blade until smooth. Serve chilled.

herb butters

ingredients

Herb butters (or margarines) are prepared in advance of serving, refrigerated, and dropped on cooked vegetables, pasta, or rice in place of the usual plain butter or margarine. They're also quite good served on steaks, fish, or poultry!

Herb butters can be frozen in a plastic ice-cube tray and popped out one portion at a time as needed. Or, refrigerate them in small containers and use them as sandwich spreads in place of mayonnaise. They can also be formed into long rolls, chilled, and sliced as needed. Directions follow.

roll in waxed paper; chill.

shaping, storage, and serving of herb butter rolls

Wrap the prepared Herb Butter in waxed paper lightly moistened with cold water. Form into a roll and chill until hard. Just before serving, remove from the refrigerator. Cut into slices with a knife that has been dipped into hot water. Place slices on crushed ice to avoid softening. Serve with steaks, poultry, fish, or vegetables.

unroll carefully.

shaping, storage, and serving of herb butters

slice with warm knife; serve on a bed of cracked ice.

19

parsley butter

Yield: About ½ cup

    ½ cup (1 stick) cold butter, cut
        into 6 pieces
    3 tablespoons fresh parsley leaves
    ⅛ teaspoon freshly ground black
        pepper

Place all ingredients in the processor bowl and process with the metal blade until parsley is finely chopped. Use with potatoes or other vegetables.

béarnaise butter

Yield: About ½ cup

    ½ cup (1 stick) cold butter, cut
        into 6 pieces
    1 teaspoon dried tarragon
    1 tablespoon dry white wine
    1 teaspoon vinegar

Combine all ingredients in the processor bowl and process with the metal blade until light. Serve with poultry, steaks, or fish.

lemon butter

Yield: About ½ cup

    ½ cup (1 stick) cold butter, cut
        into 6 pieces
    3 tablespoons fresh parsley leaves
    1 tablespoon lemon juice
    ⅛ teaspoon freshly ground black
        pepper

Place all ingredients in processor bowl and process with metal blade until parsley is minced, about 15 seconds. Serve with potatoes, fish, or in poultry sandwiches.

Picture on opposite page: herb butter served with broiled steak, garnished with lemon slices, potato sticks, and cress

ginger–green-onion butter

Yield: ½ cup

   ½ **cup (1 stick) cold butter, cut into 6 pieces**
   1 **slice fresh gingerroot, ¼ inch thick**
   1 **scallion, cut into 1-inch pieces**
   ½ **teaspoon salt**

Place butter and ginger in processor bowl and process with the metal blade until ginger is finely minced. Add scallion and salt and process until scallion is finely chopped. Serve with fish.

garlic butter (snail butter)

Yield: ½ cup

    ½ cup (1 stick) cold butter, cut
        into 6 pieces
    1 or 2 cloves garlic
    1 tablespoon fresh parsley leaves
    ½ teaspoon salt

Place butter and garlic in processor bowl and process with the metal blade until garlic is very finely minced, about 10 seconds. Add parsley and salt and process until parsley is finely chopped, about 5 seconds. Serve with vegetables or snails.

pesto sauce

Not truly a butter, but used in the same way on vegetables, rice, or pasta.

Yield: About 1½ cups

    2 cups fresh basil leaves (or fresh parsley)
    1 cup Parmesan cheese
    ½ cup olive oil

Place all ingredients in processor bowl and process with the metal blade until basil is minced. Serve with pasta or vegetables. Store covered in the refrigerator. Stir before using.

Also try the Pesto alla Genovese (see Index).

creative fines herbes butter

Yield: ½ cup

Use your favorite herbs and process with one stick of butter. Use 3 tablespoons fresh chives, rosemary, chervil, tarragon, dillweed, or coriander for each stick of butter.

Wonderful if you have an herb garden! Use 1 or 2 teaspoons dried herbs per stick of butter if fresh herbs are not available.

pasta

Pasta is the Italian word for flour paste formed into several hundred different shapes, each shape characteristic of a particular region in Italy.

Italians eat pasta as a first or second course. In America we usually serve it as a main course or in place of a starchy vegetable. The most popular pastas are spaghetti, fettuccine, and tagliatelle (about ⅛ inch narrower than fettuccine). These are served with olive oil, butter, tomato sauces, clam sauces, cheese, or herbs. The lasagna and manicotti pastas are layered with various fillings and served as oven dishes.

Your food processor enables you to prepare the pasta dough very quickly. If you have a pasta machine, shaping the noodles is fast and easy. If not, roll out the dough and cut it into the desired shapes by hand. The noodles can be cooked immediately in only a few minutes, or they can be dried and stored in airtight containers.

Sauces and fillings are also speedily prepared with the food processor.

basic pasta

Yield: About 16 ounces, or 8 servings

3 cups all-purpose flour (semolina flour is preferred, if you can obtain it)

3 eggs

2 tablespoons vegetable oil or olive oil
⅓ cup water
½ teaspoon salt

Place all ingredients in the processor bowl. Process with the metal blade until a ball forms on the blades. Remove dough, cover it, and let it rest about 30 minutes for ease in handling.

Divide the dough into 4 parts. Roll out each part paper thin and cut according to directions for form desired. Pasta may be cooked immediately or dried at room temperature overnight and stored in tightly sealed plastic bags. Noodles are very fragile and break easily.

pasta forms

fettuccine

Let the rolled-out sheets dry for 10 to 15 minutes so they won't adhere to themselves when rolled. Roll the dough tightly. Cut into ¼-inch-wide slices. Pick up and shake to loosen and unfurl.

tagliatelle

Cut dough slightly narrower than for fettuccine.

manicotti

Cut dough into 4-inch squares.

lasagna

Cut dough into strips 2 inches wide by 8 inches long.

how to cook pasta

If possible, cook pasta at once rather than let it dry. Place it in a large quantity of vigorously boiling water containing some salt and a tablespoon of oil. Oil helps to prevent boil-over and reduces the stickiness of pasta after it is cooked. Depending on the thickness, fresh pasta is cooked in 2 to 5 minutes or when it rises to the surface. It should remain slightly chewy or "al dente" to the teeth. Dried pasta requires a longer cooking time.

Drain in a colander and serve at once with sauce or use in a favorite casserole dish. Never rinse it with cold water unless you happen to enjoy cold noodles.

pasta verde (green pasta)

Yield: About 12 ounces, or 8 servings

1 10-ounce package frozen spinach, cooked, large stems removed, and squeezed very dry
2 cups all-purpose flour (use semolina flour if you can obtain it)
3 eggs
2 tablespoons vegetable oil or olive oil
½ teaspoon salt

Place spinach in the processor bowl and process with the metal blade until very finely chopped. Add remaining ingredients and proceed, following the directions for Basic Pasta.

whole-wheat pasta

Substitute whole-wheat flour for ½ of the all-purpose flour in the Basic Pasta recipe.

pesto alla genovese with pasta

pesto alla genovese

A quick and delightfully easy sauce to prepare, Pesto is great not only with pasta but with vegetables as well. It is traditionally made with fresh basil. If you do not have a fresh supply from your garden, try fresh parsley. Sauce may be refrigerated for a week, or it may be frozen. Olive oil may be substituted for butter.

Yield: 1 cup for about 1 pound cooked pasta

½ **cup cold butter, cut into 6 pieces**
1 **clove garlic**
1 **cup fresh basil or parsley leaves, loosely packed**

¼ **cup grated Parmesan cheese**
⅓ **cup pine nuts or walnuts (optional)**

Place all ingredients in the processor bowl and process with the metal blade until parsley is minced. Serve over well-drained hot pasta or with green beans, cauliflower, or baked potatoes.

If ungrated Parmesan cheese is used, cut it into small pieces before using to prevent damaging the metal blade.

25

gnocchi verdi

In Italy a small dish of pasta is served between the antipasto and the main course. These little green-and-white dumplings may substitute, on occasion, for the pasta. You may serve them as part of the main course or for lunch. They are absolutely delicious!

Yield: 30 gnocchi, 4 to 6 servings

gnocchi

1 10-ounce package frozen spinach, completely defrosted, large stems discarded, and squeezed thoroughly dry
1 pound ricotta cheese
¼ cup grated Parmesan cheese
⅓ cup all-purpose flour
2 eggs
½ teaspoon salt
¼ teaspoon freshly ground black pepper
¼ teaspoon nutmeg
½ cup or more flour for dredging

topping

3 to 4 tablespoons melted butter or cream
3 to 4 tablespoons grated Parmesan cheese

Place all ingredients for the gnocchi — spinach, cheeses, flour, eggs, and seasonings — in the processor bowl. Process with the metal blade until spinach is minced, about 6 seconds. Use at once or refrigerate for several hours.

Shape the mixture into 1½-inch balls. Roll lightly in flour. Gently drop about 12 at a time into 4 quarts of boiling water. They will sink and then rise to the surface. Cook for about 5 minutes. Remove with a slotted spoon. Keep them warm while preparing others.

Place in a greased 13 x 9-inch baking dish. Dribble with melted butter or cream, and sprinkle with Parmesan cheese. Place under the broiler until cheese begins to melt. Serve at once.

gnocchi verdi

white clam sauce

Yield: About 2 cups

    1 **scallion, cut into 1-inch pieces**
    1 **clove garlic**
    2 **tablespoons fresh parsley leaves**
    ¼ **cup olive oil**
    ¼ **cup butter**
    ⅛ **teaspoon freshly ground black pepper**
    2 **8-ounce cans minced clams, undrained**
    ¼ **cup dry white wine**

Process the scallion, garlic, and parsley with the metal blade until minced. Sauté in oil and butter until soft. Add pepper, clams, and wine. Simmer 5 minutes. Serve at once on hot pasta.

genoise sauce

Yield: 4 cups

    2 **medium onions**
    2 **stalks celery**
    1 **carrot**
    ½ **pound mushrooms**
    ½ **cup olive oil**
    1 **pound veal**
    3 **medium tomatoes, skinned**
    ¾ **cup dry red wine**
    ½ **cup beef stock or bouillon**
    ¼ **cup cold water shaken with 2 tablespoons flour until free of lumps**
Salt and pepper to taste

Coarsely chop the onions, celery, carrot, and mushrooms separately with the metal blade.

Gently cook the mushrooms in olive oil until soft, about 3 minutes. Add the celery and carrot. Cook about 5 minutes.

Coarsely chop the veal with the metal blade. Add to the vegetables and brown lightly.

Add tomatoes, wine, stock, and flour and water mixture. Season to taste. Simmer for about an hour. Serve over hot pasta.

Picture on opposite page: spaghetti alla carbonara (black-pepper spaghetti).

spaghetti alla carbonara (black-pepper spaghetti)

This is a favorite dish of one of our former Presidents. I use a pound of Italian sausage meat in place of the bacon when serving this as a main course.

Yield: 8 servings as a first course

- 1 **pound spaghetti noodles**
- 2 **cloves garlic**
- 4 **thick slices bacon, cut into cubes, or 8 ounces mild Italian sausage, casing removed**
- 3 **tablespoons butter**
- ½ **cup light cream or milk**
- 4 **eggs**
- ¼ **cup fresh parsley leaves**
- ½ **cup grated Parmesan cheese**
- ½ **teaspoon freshly grated black pepper**

Place spaghetti in a large quantity of boiling, salted water and cook, uncovered, until tender.

Meanwhile, brown bacon and garlic in butter in a skillet; remove from heat, and discard the garlic. Just before spaghetti is ready, add cream to bacon and bring to a boil.

Place eggs, parsley, cheese, and pepper in processor bowl. Process with metal blade until parsley is minced.

Drain hot spaghetti; place in a hot bowl. Add hot cream and bacon mixture and toss until combined. Add the egg mixture and toss until well mixed. Serve at once in hot bowls. Sprinkle with additional pepper and Parmesan cheese, if you like.

cannelloni

Serve with a tossed salad and dry red wine.

Yield: 4 or 5 servings

pasta

15 4½ × 5-inch paper-thin rectangles of freshly prepared pasta dough (these may be prepared in advance and refrigerated or frozen in airtight wrap, with each slice separated by a double thickness of waxed paper)

filling

2 cloves garlic
2 onions, cut into quarters
¾ pound ground beef
¼ pound mild Italian sausage, casing removed
2 tablespoons tomato paste
½ cup dry red wine

2 tablespoons fresh parsley leaves, chopped
⅛ teaspoon freshly ground black pepper
1 teaspoon oregano
½ teaspoon thyme
1 teaspoon salt

cut pasta dough into 4½ x 5-inch rectangles.

prepare filling.

fill pasta; roll firmly and seal.

boil cannelloni 10 minutes.

prepare sauce.

cover boiled cannelloni with sauce and parmesan cheese.

sauce

- 1 onion, quartered
- 2 cloves garlic
- 2 ounces slab bacon, cubed
- 2 large tomatoes, peeled and quartered
- ¼ pound mushrooms, sliced with the slicing disk into "T" shapes
- 3 tablespoons tomato paste
- 3 tablespoons dry red wine
- Salt and pepper to taste

garnish

- 2 tablespoons grated Parmesan cheese
- 2 tablespoons butter or margarine

Prepare the filling. Chop the garlic and onion with the metal blade. Brown in a skillet with beef and sausage. Add remaining filling ingredients. Place some of the filling in the center of each pasta rectangle. Roll firmly and seal the seam and ends with a little water. Drop filled pasta in boiling salted water for about 10 minutes. Remove with a slotted spoon and place seam side down in a greased baking dish.

Prepare the sauce. Chop the garlic and onion with the metal blade. Place in a skillet with the bacon and cook over moderate heat until bacon is browned. Chop the tomatoes with the metal blade. Add to the bacon mixture along with the remaining sauce ingredients. Simmer 20 minutes.

Pour sauce over rolls. Top with Parmesan cheese; dot with butter. Bake at 400°F for about 15 minutes or until heated through.

This dish may be prepared in advance and refrigerated. Increase baking time to 30 to 40 minutes.

Picture on opposite page: preparation of cannelloni

Picture on next page: cannelloni.

ravioli

Yield: About 8 servings

1 recipe Basic Pasta
Desired filling

Divide pasta dough into 4 parts. On a floured surface roll out 1 part into a paper-thin square. Mark off 1½-inch squares lightly with a knife and trim off extra dough. Place a heaping teaspoon of cheese or beef filling in the center of each square; flatten slightly. Roll out a second square of dough, a little larger than the first. Lightly moisten the borders between the squares on the filled dough and cover with the second square. Press between the filling, lengthwise and crosswise. Cut between the squares with a pizza cutter or fluted pastry wheel. Separate squares and seal edges with the tines of a fork. Repeat with remaining dough. Let ravioli stand to dry for 1 hour before cooking.

Cook in boiling salted water for 5 to 7 minutes, until tender. Drain. Serve at once with melted butter and grated Parmesan cheese or your favorite pasta sauce.

ravioli

beef ravioli filling

Yield: About 3 cups

- ½ pound Italian sweet sausage
- ½ pound lean ground beef
- 2 medium onions, quartered, and chopped with the metal blade
- ¼ cup parsley leaves, chopped with the metal blade
- 1 1-pound can tomatoes
- 1 clove garlic

Salt and pepper to taste

Combine the sausage meat, beef, and onions in a frying pan. Sauté until meat is browned. Drain. Add remaining ingredients. Simmer for 30 minutes or until thick.

Place mixture in processor bowl and process with the metal blade until blended, about 6 seconds. Refrigerate until ready for use.

cheese ravioli filling

Yield: 3 to 4 cups

- 1 10-ounce package frozen, defrosted spinach, stems discarded, and squeezed thoroughly dry
- or ¾ pound fresh spinach, steamed 5 minutes, stems discarded, and squeezed thoroughly dry
- 1 pound ricotta cheese
- ½ cup Parmesan cheese
- ¼ teaspoon nutmeg
- 1 teaspoon basil
- 2 eggs

Place all ingredients in processor bowl and process with the metal blade until smooth, about 7 seconds. Refrigerate or use at once.

main dishes

german quiche

Very good and very filling.

Yield: 4 to 6 servings

    1 recipe Pâté Brisée (see Index)
        pastry crust
    5 bacon slices, cut into quarters,
        lightly browned, and drained
    8 or 9 ounces Swiss or cheddar
        cheese shredded with the
        shredding disk
    1 cup milk or light cream
    3 eggs
    Dash pepper and nutmeg

Pat pastry into a 10-inch quiche mold or a 9-inch pie pan. Distribute bacon over crust.

Combine remaining ingredients in processor bowl, using metal or plastic blade. Pour over the bacon into the crust. A few thin slices of cheese may be arranged over the surface. Bake at 375° F for 30 minutes. Serve warm.

calzone italiana

Follow the recipe for Calzone alla Napoli and use the following filling in place of the ham-and-cheese filling.

Yield: 4 or 5 servings

    1 pound mild Italian sausage,
        casing removed
    2 teaspoons oregano
    1 8-ounce can tomato sauce
    8 ounces mozzarella cheese,
        shredded with the shredding
        disk
    1 cup grated Parmesan cheese

Brown the sausage in a skillet. Drain well. Add oregano and tomato sauce. Spread on turnovers, top with cheeses, seal, and bake as directed.

banana meat loaf

Cooked carrots, frankfurters, or small pickles may be used in place of the bananas.

Yield: 4 or 5 servings

- **1 pound lean beef, cut into 1-inch cubes**
- **2 onions, each cut into quarters**
- **2 tablespoons fresh parsley leaves**
- **2 eggs**
- **1 teaspoon salt**
- **¼ teaspoon freshly ground pepper**
- **2 cups cooked rice**
- **2 bananas, peeled**

Process half the beef, onions, parsley, eggs, salt, and pepper at a time in the processor bowl, using the metal blade, turning it on and off quickly, until the beef and onions are coarsely chopped.

Add this mixture to the rice and mix well. Place half of mixture in the bottom of a 9 × 5-inch loaf pan. Place bananas on top. Cover with remaining meat mixture. Bake at 350° F for about 1 hour. Serve at once.

banana meat loaf

Picture on opposite page:
german quiche

turkish meatball kebabs

turkish meatball kebabs

Yield: 4 servings

- **1 pound lean beef or lamb cut into 1-inch cubes**
- **2 small boiled potatoes, peeled**
- **2 small onions, each cut into quarters**
- **1 small green pepper, seeded and cut into 8 pieces**
- **4 sprigs fresh parsley leaves**
- **1 teaspoon salt**
- **1 teaspoon prepared mustard**
- **1 teaspoon curry powder (optional)**
- **Flour for rolling**
- **Vegetable oil for frying**

Process half of the ingredients at a time in the processor bowl with the metal blade, turning it on and off quickly, until meat and vegetables are coarsely chopped.

Form plum-size meatballs. Roll in flour. Fry in a small amount of oil in a skillet, or deep fry in oil at 375° F until done. Remove and drain well. Serve on 4 wooden skewers.

joan's swiss-cheese fondue

The food processor is a great help during the preparation of cheese fondues. Often a large quantity of cheese must be grated, and this step is done rapidly with the shredding disk.

Yield: 4 servings

- **1 pound Swiss cheese, shredded with the shredding disk**
- **1½ cups dry white table wine**
- **1 clove garlic**
- **2 tablespoons cornstarch**
- **Dash of freshly ground black pepper**
- **Dash of nutmeg**
- **2 tablespoons kirsch**
- **1-inch cubes of stale French or Italian bread**

Combine cheese, wine, garlic, cornstarch, pepper, and nutmeg in a fondue or chafing dish. Heat gently, stirring occasionally, just until mixture thickens and begins to bubble. Remove garlic clove and discard. Stir in kirsch. Spear bread cubes on fondue forks and dunk bread into fondue. Keep heat under fondue low to prevent coagulation of the cheese.

Joan's swiss-cheese fondue

california stuffed breast of veal

Yield: 6 servings

stuffing

- 1 **pound fresh spinach, large stems removed**
- 1 **medium onion, quartered**
- 3 **tablespoons butter or margarine**
- ⅔ **cup raisins, plumped in boiling water, then drained**
- ¼ **cup bread crumbs (or 1 slice dry bread, quartered, and chopped with the metal blade)**
- 1 **teaspoon salt**
- 1 **teaspoon basil**
- 1 **teaspoon parsley**
- 1 **egg yolk**

veal breast

- 1 **4- to 4½- pound breast of veal**
- **Salt and pepper**
- 3 **to 4 tablespoons vegetable oil**
- ½ **cup dry white wine**
- 2 **bay leaves**
- 4 **whole cloves**
- ¼ **cup hot beef broth, if needed**

Prepare the stuffing. Wash spinach well and shred with the slicing disk. Chop the onion with the metal blade. Sauté the onions in butter in a large skillet until soft. Add the spinach and sauté until just wilted. Remove from heat. Add raisins, bread crumbs, seasonings, and the egg yolk. Toss until combined.

Prepare the veal breast. Remove breastbone, ribs, and cartilage from veal breast with sharp knife. Cut pocket in meat, season with salt and pepper, and fill with stuffing. Close pocket with toothpicks. Heat oil in a large skillet. Brown stuffed breasts on all sides for about 15 minutes. Lower heat and add wine, bay leaves, and cloves. Cover and simmer over low heat for about 2 hours. Add broth if necessary to replenish liquid in bottom of pan. Baste meat occasionally.

Serve at once on a hot platter. Remove toothpicks and slice the meat.

Picture on opposite page: California stuffed breast of veal

stuffed chicken breasts

Yield: 4 to 8 servings

5 ounces lean veal	4 ounces canned mushrooms, drained
5 ounces lean pork	4 whole chicken breasts
3 ounces chicken giblets or liver	Butter for frying
1 slice stale bread, torn in quarters	½ cup water
3 eggs	½ cup sour cream
½ teaspoon salt	1 tablespoon cornstarch
2 tablespoons fresh parsley leaves	

Coarsely chop veal, pork, and giblets with the metal blade. Remove to a large bowl.

Combine bread, eggs, salt, parsley, and mushrooms in processor bowl. Process with metal blade until mushrooms are finely chopped. Add to meat.

Bone the chicken breasts, keeping each breast in one piece. Fill the breasts with the meat mixture. Sew or fasten with skewers to close. Fry in butter until browned on all sides. Add water, cover, and cook 30 minutes. Remove chicken and keep it warm.

Add sour cream and cornstarch to drippings. Heat until thick. Serve over chicken on a bed of sauerkraut.

Picture on next pages: stuffed chicken breasts   41

seafood tempura

Yield: 6 to 8 servings

frying batter

> 1 large egg
> ¾ cup water
> 1 cup sifted all-purpose flour
> ½ teaspoon salt
> 1 teaspoon rosemary
> 1 teaspoon basil

seafood

> Vegetable oil for deep-fat frying
> ½ pound sliced eel
> ½ pound shrimps
> ½ pound mussels
> ½ pound fish fillets, rolled and
>   fastened with toothpicks

Combine ingredients for batter in processor bowl and process with metal blade just until smooth. Let batter stand for 1 hour, or refrigerate it overnight. This thickens the batter and softens the flour.

Heat oil to 400° F. Using tongs, dip seafood pieces into batter, drain briefly, and drop gently into hot fat. Deep-fry until brown, about 3 or 4 minutes, depending on size of seafood pieces. Remove from oil as done and drain on paper toweling. Serve with assorted dips for seafood.

baked fish in foil with herb butter

Yield: 2 to 3 servings per pound of fish used

> 1 whole fish, entrails and scales
>   removed
> 2 slices orange
> Fresh parsley sprigs
> Fresh dillweed sprigs
> 3 thick slices of a favorite Herb
>   Butter* (see Contents)
> Aluminum foil

Wrap fish in aluminum foil after topping with remaining ingredients. Bake at 400° F for about 15 minutes per pound. Serve at once.

Fish may be stuffed before baking with a variation of Basic Bread Stuffing (see Index).

*Parsley, Lemon, Béarnaise, etc.

Picture on opposite page: seafood tempura

scalloped fish

Yield: 4 servings

4 baking shells or ramekins

fish

1 tablespoon lemon juice
1 pound fish fillets
2 bay leaves
4 whole cloves
6 whole peppercorns
1 small onion, sliced

bechamel sauce

2 tablespoons butter
1 onion, chopped with
the metal blade
2 tablespoons flour
1 cup fish broth
½ teaspoon salt
⅛ teaspoon nutmeg
¼ teaspoon paprika
⅛ teaspoon pepper
4 blades chives, cut into
¼-inch pieces
½ cup light cream

garnish

4 tablespoons Parmesan cheese
1 slice stale bread, crumbled with the metal blade
2 tablespoons butter

scalloped fish

Sprinkle lemon juice over fish; let stand for 10 minutes. Place fish in a wire basket and poach in simmering water to cover with the bay leaves, cloves, peppercorns, and onion for about 10 to 15 minutes. Remove fish and let it drain, reserving broth. Place fish in processor bowl and process with metal blade by turning on and off quickly until fish is coarsely chopped.

Prepare the sauce. Place butter in a skillet and cook the onion until it is soft. Add flour and blend with butter until no lumps remain. Add 1 cup of the reserved fish broth gradually, stirring constantly. Add salt and spices. Bring to a boil. Add chives and cream.

Fill shells or ramekins with fish. Pour sauce over each. Sprinkle with Parmesan cheese and bread crumbs; dot with butter. Bake at 400° F for about 15 minutes. Serve at once.

italian beans

Serve this tasty combination of cheese, vegetables, beans, and spices in place of meat. When I teach a class in vegetarian cooking, I always have the students prepare this recipe. Everyone enjoys it each time it is made.

Yield: 4 servings

2 large onions, quartered
2 cloves garlic
2 tablespoons vegetable oil
1 large stalk celery, cut into 3-inch lengths
⅔ cup fresh parsley leaves
2 tomatoes, quartered
2 carrots

1½ cups canned kidney beans (1 pound) and half the can liquid
5 teaspoons dried basil
1 teaspoon oregano
2 teaspoons salt
Pepper to taste
4 ounces cheddar cheese

Insert the metal blade in the processor bowl and coarsely chop the onions. Finely chop the garlic. Sauté both in vegetable oil until tender.

Separately chop the celery, parsley leaves, and tomatoes coarsely with the metal blade.

Grate the carrots with the shredding disk. Add these vegetables, beans and liquid, spices, salt and pepper to the onion and garlic. Heat. Vegetables should remain rather crisp. Sprinkle with cheese, shredded with the shredding disk. Serve at once with boiled brown rice.

stuffed zucchini

Yield: 4 servings

4 medium zucchini
Salt and pepper
1 pound cubed lamb, chopped with the metal blade 1 cup at a time
2 tomatoes, coarsely chopped with metal blade

¼ cup frozen, defrosted peas
½ cup boiled rice
1 cup hot beef broth or bouillon
4 ounces Swiss cheese, shredded with the shredding disk

Wash and trim ends from zucchini. Cook in boiling water 5 minutes. Halve lengthwise and scoop out seeds with a spoon. Season halves with salt and pepper.

Brown the lamb in a skillet. Drain, and add tomatoes, peas, and rice. Season to taste with salt and pepper. Fill zucchini halves with mixture. Place in a casserole dish. Add broth, and cover. Bake at 350°F for 20 minutes. Uncover. Top with cheese and bake 10 minutes longer, uncovered. Serve at once.

teriyaki meatballs

teriyaki meatballs

Yield: 4 servings

meatballs

- ¼ cup fresh parsley leaves
- 2 stalks celery with leaves, cut into 1-inch pieces
- 1 slice bread, torn into 4 pieces
- ½ teaspoon salt
- 1 egg
- 1 pound cubed lean beef, chopped 1 cup at a time, using the metal blade

gravy

- ⅓ cup cold water mixed with 1 tablespoon cornstarch
- ¼ cup soy sauce
- ½ teaspoon paprika
- 1 teaspoon sugar
- ¼ teaspoon ground ginger
- 2 tablespoons candied fruit

Place parsley, celery, bread, salt, and egg in processor bowl. Process with metal blade until celery is finely chopped.

Add to meat and form mixture into walnut-sized balls. Brown in hot oil in a skillet for 5 minutes. Drain.

Heat ingredients for gravy in a saucepan until mixture boils and is clear. Pour over meatballs. Serve hot with boiled rice. Garnish with celery leaves.

48

calzone alla napoli
(ham and cheese turnovers)

Serve these with wine and a tossed salad for a light supper.

Yield: 10 rolls, to serve 4 or 5

dough

1 recipe White Bread dough or 1 10 ounce can refrigerated Parker House rolls

filling

8 ounces mozzarella cheese
½ pound cooked ham, cut into
    1-inch cubes
10 green olives, pitted
Salt and pepper to taste
1 egg white
1 to 2 tablespoons milk

Divide dough into 10 pieces. Roll out each on a floured surface to 5-inch-round circles.

Grate cheese with shredding disk. Chop ham and olives with metal blade. Combine ham, olives, and cheese. Season with salt and pepper. Place mixture on half of each dough circle to within ¼ inch of edge. Brush edges with egg white. Fold plain half over and seal. Place on a greased baking sheet; brush each turnover with milk. Bake at 400° F for 15 to 20 minutes. Serve at once.

calzone alla napoli (ham and cheese turnovers)

vegetables

baked butternut squash and apples

Roast seeds (see Roasted Pumpkin Seeds in the recipe that follows) for a high protein snack.

Yield: 6 servings

1 small (2-pound) butternut squash, pared, seeded, and cut into pieces to fit tube
2 apples, cored and cut into quarters
½ cup brown sugar
¼ cup cold butter or margarine, cut into 5 pieces
1 tablespoon flour
1 teaspoon salt
¼ teaspoon cinnamon
¼ teaspoon nutmeg

Slice squash and apples with the slicing disk, using firm pressure on the pusher. Place in a rectangular baking dish.

Process remaining ingredients with metal blade until blended. Sprinkle over apples and squash. Cover with foil and bake at 350°F until tender, about 50 minutes.

pureed pumpkin and roasted pumpkin seeds

Yield: About 3 or 4 cups pureed pumpkin

Remove the seeds and strands from an 8-inch pumpkin and set aside. Cut pumpkin into 3-inch squares and peel outer skin from each. Steam, using a small amount of water, for 30 minutes or until pieces are very tender. Drain well.

Place pumpkin in processor bowl and process with metal blade until smooth.

To roast seeds, remove strands from seeds and discard. Do not wash or rinse seeds. Spread on a baking sheet and sprinkle with salt. Bake at 350° F for 20 minutes; stir occasionally.

sliced carrots with honey and parsley

Yield: 4 servings

> 6 **medium carrots, scraped**
> 2 **tablespoons fresh parsley leaves**
> 2 **tablespoons butter or margarine**
> 2 **tablespoons honey**

Wedge the carrots into the tube and slice with the slicing disk, using firm pressure on the pusher. Chop the parsley with the metal blade.

Place carrots and parsley in a saucepan with a small amount of water. Dot with butter and dribble with honey. Steam over moderate heat until tender.

To prepare in a microwave oven, use a small glass casserole dish and cook for 5 minutes.

mashed potatoes

Yield: 4 servings

> 4 **boiled, skinned potatoes**
> 2 **tablespoons butter or margarine**
> **Salt and freshly ground pepper to taste**
> ¼ **cup milk**

Place all ingredients in processor bowl and process with metal blade until smooth. Serve at once, garnished with parsley leaves and paprika.

scalloped potatoes

Yield: 4 or 5 servings

> 4 **medium potatoes, peeled, and**
>   **sliced with the slicing disk**
> 1 **medium onion, sliced with the**
>   **slicing disk**
> **Salt and freshly ground black**
>   **pepper**
> **About 2 cups milk**
> 2 **tablespoons butter or margarine**

Layer the potato and onion slices in a greased baking dish. Season each layer with salt and pepper. Add milk to within ½ inch from the top. Dot with butter and bake, uncovered, at 350° F for 1¼ hours.

baked potatoes with sour cream and caviar

Yield: 6 to 8 servings

> **6 to 8 medium baking potatoes, baked**
> **½ pint sour cream**
> **1 small pickle, cut into 1-inch pieces**
> **1 small onion, quartered**
> **1 sprig fresh dillweed or parsley**
> **⅛ teaspoon freshly ground black pepper**
> **½ teaspoon salt**
> **Caviar for garnishing**

Cut crisscross across the top of the baked potatoes. Press the sides to split the cross open and expose the insides of the potatoes.

Place sour cream, pickle, onion, dill, pepper, and salt in processor bowl and process with metal blade until pickle and onion are coarsely chopped. Spoon mixture onto potatoes. Garnish with caviar and additional sprigs of dill or parsley.

golden sweet potatoes

A must for Thanksgiving dinner, these sweet potatoes are laced with sherry and orange juice. Leftovers freeze well. Double the recipe for a large group and process half at a time.

Yield: 4 to 6 servings

> **2 pounds sweet potatoes (4 medium)**
> **1 teaspoon cinnamon**
> **1 teaspoon salt**

> **2 tablespoons brown sugar**
> **2 tablespoons butter or margarine**
> **3 tablespoons dry sherry**
> **3 tablespoons orange juice**

Boil sweet potatoes until easily pierced with a fork. Slip off and discard skins. Place potatoes in processor bowl with remaining ingredients. Process with metal blade until smooth; scrape down sides and break up large pieces with spatula, if necessary.

Heap into a 1-quart casserole dish. Dot with additional butter and bake at 350°F until reheated. This dish may be prepared in advance and refrigerated.

If serving this with turkey, rewarm it in the oven with the turkey for about 20 to 25 minutes.

tortillas, tostadas, and tacos

You must use Masa Harina, available in most supermarkets, to make really good corn tortillas. The Quaker Oats Company makes it from ground, parched, lime-treated corn. It is milled especially for use in tortillas and tamales. If your supermarket does not carry it, the manager can order it for you. Canned or frozen tortillas are neither as tender nor as flavorful as those you prepare yourself.

Tortillas are surprisingly quick and easy to prepare and are the basis for many delectable Mexican dishes — so of course they themselves should be the best you can make or obtain. Mix them quickly in your food processor.

corn tortillas

Yield: 12 6-inch tortillas

2 cups Masa Harina (Quaker Oats Company)
1 cup cold water

Place Masa and cold water in processor bowl and process with the metal blade until smooth, about 5 seconds. Form dough into a ball, cover, and let rest for 20 to 30 minutes.

Divide dough into 12 balls. Place each ball on a surface sprinkled with more Masa, cover with waxed paper, and roll into a 6-inch circle. Peel off waxed paper and transfer with a wide spatula to an ungreased frypan. Heat over moderate heat about 1 minute per side. Turn when edges are dry. The centers should remain soft. Stack them on a warm dish and cover with a towel.

Tortillas may be refrigerated and rewarmed by wrapping them in foil and heating in a warm oven (250°F) for about 4 to 5 minutes.

Use these tortillas to prepare Tostados and Tacos. Use them also to prepare Corn Chips, recipe given elsewhere in this book (see Index).

tostados

These crisp, fried tortillas are used as the basis for open-faced Mexican sandwiches.

Yield: 12 tostados

12 Tortillas (see preceding recipe), dried at room temperature for several hours
Vegetable oil for frying

Heat about ½ to 1 inch of oil in a frying pan to 350°F. Fry each tortilla until lightly browned, crisp around the edges, but still soft in the centers — 1 minute or less. Drain on paper towels. Keep them warm in a 200° oven.

If these become too crisp, they will crack in half when topped with heavy fillings.

Picture on opposite page: baked potatoes with sour cream and caviar

flour tortillas

Used for chimichangas.

Yield: 10 7-inch tortillas

3 cups all-purpose flour
¼ cup cold lard or hydrogenated
    shortening, cut into 4 pieces
½ teaspoon salt
1 cup water

Place flour, shortening, and salt in processor bowl. Process with metal blade until the consistency of cornmeal. Add water and process until a ball forms on the blades or the motor begins to stall, about 5 seconds.

Knead dough on a floured surface for 3 to 4 minutes. Cover and let rest for 20 to 30 minutes.

Divide dough into 10 balls. Roll out each between 2 sheets of waxed paper to a 7-inch circle. Peel off the top sheet and invert into a preheated, ungreased frying pan. Heat, peel off top paper; turn when lightly browned, and brown the other side.

Serve at once or wrap in aluminum foil and refrigerate. Rewarm the package in a 250°F oven for 4 to 5 minutes.

chalupas (nuevo león style)

Yield: 8

8 Tostados
1 16-ounce can refried beans or 2
    cups Refried Beans (recipe
    follows), heated in a saucepan
    over moderate heat

6 ounces cheddar cheese, shredded
    with the shredding disk
10 leaves romaine lettuce, thinly
    sliced with the slicing disk
1 large tomato, chopped with the
    metal blade

toppings

Hot Taco Sauce (recipe follows), or
    use bottled taco sauce
Guacamole Topping (recipe
    follows)
Sour cream

Chalupas may be prepared in the kitchen and served already assembled, or the ingredients may be placed on the table and each guest assemble his own.

Spread each tostado with refried beans. Top with cheese, lettuce, then chopped tomato. Add a spoonful of Guacamole or sour cream and a little Hot Taco Sauce.

chicken chalupas

Prepare Chalupas as directed, but add about 1 cup of cooked chicken, chopped coarsely with the metal blade, as a topping on the lettuce.

taco shells

Yield: 12

Vegetable oil for frying
12 freshly prepared Tortillas

Heat ½ to 1 inch of oil in a frying pan to 350° F. Fry each tortilla until it becomes soft, 2 to 3 seconds. With tongs, fold it in half, leaving a space for a filling, and continue to fry until lightly browned, less than 1 minute. Drain on paper towels and keep warm in a 200° F oven.

tacos

Yield: 12 tacos

12 Taco Shells

meat filling

- 1 small onion
- 1 clove garlic
- ½ green pepper, cut in 3 pieces
- ½ pound ground beef
- ½ pound pork sausage
- 1 8-ounce can tomato sauce
- 2 teaspoons chili powder
- 1 teaspoon salt

toppings

- 4 to 6 ounces cheddar cheese, shredded with the shredding disk
- 8 to 10 leaves romaine lettuce, sliced with the slicing disk
- 2 tomatoes, quartered, and chopped coarsely with the metal blade
- Guacamole Topping (see Index)
- Hot Taco Sauce (see Index), or use bottled taco sauce

Prepare the meat filling by coarsely chopping the onion, garlic, and green pepper in the processor bowl with the metal blade. Place in a skillet with the ground beef and sausage. Sauté until the meat is brown. Drain well. Add the tomato sauce, chili powder, and salt. Simmer 10 to 15 minutes to let the flavors blend.

Fill the taco shells with the meat mixture. Top with cheese, lettuce, and tomatoes. Serve at once with Guacamole Topping and Hot Taco Sauce.

hot taco sauce

Serve with Tacos or Chalupas.

Yield: ½ cup

1 to 2 medium tomatoes
1 small onion
2 or 3 mild chili peppers, canned
or fresh

1 teaspoon vinegar
½ teaspoon salt
¼ cup water
½ teaspoon corriander or oregano

Place all ingredients in processor bowl and process with metal blade until coarsely chopped. Refrigerate for about an hour before serving. Serve cold or at room temperature.

refried beans

Yield: 2 cups

1 small onion, halved, or 2
scallions, cut into 1-inch
pieces

¼ cup lard
2 cups cooked pinto or pink beans

Chop the onion in the processor bowl with the metal blade and cook in lard until soft. Do not brown.

Puree the beans in the food processor with the metal blade and add to the onion. Cook and stir constantly until the beans are thick and begin to dry and brown. Use at once or freeze.

guacamole topping

Yield: ½ cup

1 very ripe, soft avocado, peeled
and pitted
½ small onion
½ teaspoon salt (or more)

½ teaspoon lemon juice
1 medium tomato, quartered
(optional)

Guacamole may be prepared smooth-style or chunky-style.

Place all ingredients, except the tomato, in the processor bowl. Process with the metal blade until smooth. Add tomato, if you wish, and process just until it is chopped. Or, place all ingredients in the processor bowl and process just until coarsely chopped.

Serve at once, as the avocados darken quickly when exposed to the air. Use as a topping for Tacos or Chalupas.

cornmeal tortillas

Make these *only* if you cannot obtain Masa Harina. They will not be as tender or as flavorful as those made from corn flour.

Yield: 12 tortillas

1 cup all-purpose flour	2 tablespoons vegetable oil
½ cup cornmeal	½ cup water
½ teaspoon salt	

Place all ingredients in the processor bowl and process with the metal blade until a ball forms on the blades. Knead on a floured surface for 2 minutes. Cover and let rest for 20 minutes for ease in handling.

Form into 12 balls. Roll out into 6-inch circles on a surface sprinkled with cornmeal. Lift with a spatula to a preheated, ungreased frying pan. Heat at 350° F for about 1 minute per side, until speckled brown, a little bubbly, and dry around the edges.

Stack on a warm dish and cover until all are done. Use at once or cover tightly and refrigerate.

Rewarm by wrapping in foil and heating in a 250° F oven for 4 to 5 minutes.

chimichangas

Yield: 4

4 Flour Tortillas (see Index)

chicken–almond filling

2 tablespoons butter or margarine
2 tablespoons flour
½ teaspoon salt
1 cup milk
8 ounces cooked chicken (2 cups), very coarsely chopped with the metal blade
1 cup blanched almonds, coarsely chopped with the metal blade

topping

6 romaine lettuce leaves, sliced with the slicing disk
1 cup radishes, sliced with the slicing disk
2 ounces Muenster or Monterrey Jack cheese, shredded with the shredding disk

Combine the butter, flour, and salt in a saucepan over moderate heat. Stir in milk and heat and stir until thick. Add chicken; heat through. Stir in the chopped almonds. At once spoon the chicken mixture into the center of each of the flour tortillas. Top with lettuce, radishes, and cheese. Wrap the tortilla around the filling. Serve immediately. Tostados or taco shells may be used in place of the flour tortillas, if you wish.

fondue dips, sauces, and relishes

paprika fondue dip

Yield: 1 cup

> ½ cup mayonnaise
> 1 tablespoon paprika
> Salt and pepper to taste
> ½ green or red pepper, cut into 4
>   pieces

Place all ingredients in processor bowl and process with metal blade until pepper is minced. Garnish with additional chopped green pepper. Serve with seafood or poultry fondue.

mushroom fondue dip

Yield: About ¾ cup

> ½ cup mayonnaise or sour cream
> 1 teaspoon lemon juice
> Dash Tabasco sauce
> Salt and pepper to taste
> ¼ cup canned mushrooms,
>   drained, or ½ cup fresh
>   chopped mushrooms browned
>   in butter
> Salt and pepper to taste

Place all ingredients in processor bowl and process with metal blade until mushrooms are coarsely chopped. Garnish with whole mushrooms.

avocado fondue dip

Yield: About 1 cup

2 ripe avocados, pitted and peeled
2 tablespoons mayonnaise
1 tablespoon lemon juice
1 teaspoon prepared mustard
Garlic salt and pepper to taste

Combine all ingredients in processor bowl and process with metal blade until smooth. Garnish with strips of lemon peel. Serve with beef, seafood, or poultry fondue.

sour-cream–chive fondue dip

Yield: About 1 cup

½ pint sour cream
1 teaspoon lemon juice
1 teaspoon prepared mustard
5 blades chives, cut into 1-inch
    pieces
Dash sugar
1 tablespoon catsup
Salt and pepper to taste

Place all ingredients in processor bowl and process with metal blade until chives are just minced. Serve with beef fondue.

onion–parsley fondue dip

Yield: About ¾ cup

¼ cup vegetable oil
1 tablespoon lemon juice
1 teaspoon prepared mustard
2 medium onions, quartered
1 tablespoon prepared horseradish
¼ cup fresh parsley leaves
½ teaspoon sugar
Salt and pepper to taste

Place all ingredients in processor bowl and process with metal blade until onion is finely chopped. Garnish with additional parsley. Especially good for beef fondue.

Picture on next pages: dips for beef or seafood fondue (clockwise from top) onion-parsley fondue dip, sour-cream-chive fondue dip, avocado fondue dip, paprika fondue dip, mushroom fondue dip

béarnaise sauce

A sure hit when served with beef fondue. My guests always enjoy this sauce. Be sure to use butter!

Yield: 1½ cups

> 2 **tablespoons dry white wine**
> **(Chablis)**
> 1 **tablespoon white vinegar**
> 2 **teaspoons chopped onion**
> ½ **teaspoon dried tarragon**
> 1 **cup butter (½ pound)**
> 3 **egg yolks**
> 1 **tablespoon water**
> **Dash cayenne pepper**

Combine the wine, vinegar, onion, and tarragon in a saucepan. Heat and reduce to 1 tablespoon. Add butter and heat until bubbly; do not brown.

Place egg yolks, water, and pepper in processor bowl. Process with the metal blade until light, about 15 seconds. Dribble the hot butter (it must be hot or it will not thicken the egg yolks) through the tube with the motor running. Add slowly, drop by drop, at first. Then add remainder in a scant, steady stream. Serve at once while warm, or chill and serve cold with steak or pot roast.

mayonnaise

Yield: 1¼ cups

> 1 **egg**
> 1 **tablespoon vinegar or lemon**
> **juice**
> ½ **teaspoon salt or a mixture of**
> **garlic and onion salt (use less**
> **if mayonnaise is to be used**
> **with salty ingredients, such as**
> **tuna)**
> ¼ **teaspoon dry mustard**
> 1 **cup vegetable oil**

Place the egg, vinegar, salt, and dry mustard in processor bowl. Process with metal blade 4 or 5 seconds. With the motor running, pour oil through the feed tube, drop by drop at first, then in a scant, steady stream. (Let it run down the edge of the bowl next to the handle.) Refrigerate in a covered jar. Use within 1 to 2 weeks.

If the mayonnaise should separate, place another egg in the processor bowl and add the separated mixture very slowly through the tube with the blades running. It will re-emulsify.

Picture on previous pages: meat sauce (counterclockwise from top) tartar sauce, horseradish sauce, gloucester sauce, tomato-wine sauce, cambridge sauce

mayonnaise variations

anchovy mayonnaise

Reduce salt in recipe and add 4 to 6 anchovy fillets with egg. Proceed as recipe directs.

garlic mayonnaise

Add 1 to 3 cloves garlic to mayonnaise. Process with metal blade until garlic is finely minced. Serve with meats, beef fondue, or sandwiches. This has a very strong, hot, garlic flavor.

green goddess dressing

Add ½ cup sour cream, 3 tablespoons fresh parsley leaves, 1 to 2 scallions cut into 1-inch pieces, and 1 to 2 anchovy fillets to mayonnaise. Process with metal blade until smooth.

herb mayonnaise

Add ½ cup fresh parsley leaves to mayonnaise. Process with metal blade until parsley is finely chopped. Scallions, fresh tarragon, and fresh dill leaves may be added with parsley.

russian dressing

Add 2 tablespoons catsup and 2 tablespoons relish or chili sauce to mayonnaise.

sauce remoulade

Reduce salt and add 1 scallion, cut into 1-inch pieces, or 1 clove garlic; 1 hard cooked egg, halved; 1 to 2 anchovy fillets; 1 tablespoon capers; 2 tablespoons fresh green herbs (parsley, chives, tarragon) to mayonnaise. Process with metal blade until smooth. Serve with fish, seafood, or lettuce.

tartar sauce

Add ¼ cup fresh parsley, 1 tablespoon capers, and 4 gherkin pickles to mayonnaise. Process with metal blade until ingredients are finely chopped.

tomato–wine sauce

Yield: About 1 cup

> ½ cup sour cream or mayonnaise
> ¼ cup tomato paste
> 2 tablespoons dry white wine
> 2 teaspoons lemon juice
> Salt and pepper to taste
> Dash Worcestershire sauce

Place all ingredients in processor bowl and process with metal blade until smooth. Serve with beef, pork, fish, or with seafood or beef fondue.

cambridge sauce

Yield: About ⅔ cup

- ½ cup sour cream or mayonnaise
- 2 hard-cooked egg yolks
- 2 teaspoons prepared mustard
- 2 anchovy fillets
- 1 tablespoon fresh parsley leaves
- ¼ teaspoon tarragon
- 3 blades chives, cut into 1-inch pieces
- Salt and pepper to taste
- Dash wine vinegar

Place all ingredients in processor bowl and process with metal blade just until anchovy fillets are coarsely chopped. Garnish with parsley or other fresh herbs and additional anchovy fillets. Serve with meat, poultry, or beef fondue.

gloucester sauce

Yield: About 1 cup

- ½ cup yogurt
- ½ cup mayonnaise
- Salt and pepper to taste
- ½ teaspoon sugar
- 1 teaspoon lemon juice
- Dash Worcestershire sauce

Place all ingredients in processor bowl and process with metal blade until smooth. Garnish with a little grated lemon rind. Serve with meat, fish, poultry, or beef fondue.

horseradish sauce

Yield: About ⅔ cup

- ½ cup mayonnaise
- 1 tablespoon prepared horseradish
- 2 tablespoons dry white wine
- ½ teaspoon sugar
- Salt and pepper to taste
- 1 peeled tomato, quartered, and coarsely chopped with metal blade

Combine all ingredients except tomatoes in processor bowl. Process with metal blade until smooth. Fold in tomato pieces and reserve a few for a garnish. Serve with meat or beef fondue.

hollandaise sauce

An indispensable sauce for broccoli, asparagus, and eggs benedict.

Yield: 1 cup

2 tablespoons lemon juice
3 egg yolks
¼ teaspoon salt
½ cup butter

Place lemon juice, egg yolks, and salt in the processor bowl. Process with metal blade until blended, about 15 seconds.

Heat butter in saucepan until bubbly; do not brown. With processor running, add the hot butter through the tube, drop by drop at first. Then add remainder in a scant, steady stream. The butter must be hot to thicken the yolks. Serve at once, or chill and serve cold over well-drained vegetables.

speedy chutney

Yield: 2 cups

½ small lemon, seeded, and cut
into 4 pieces
1 small onion, quartered
2 apples, cored, unpeeled, and cut
into 6 pieces
½ cup raisins
2 tablespoons candied citron or
mixed candied fruit
½ cup vinegar
⅔ cup brown sugar
½ teaspoon salt
½ teaspoon ginger
¼ teaspoon cinnamon
⅛ teaspoon cloves

Place lemon in processor bowl and process with metal blade until finely chopped. Add onion and process until coarsely chopped; add apples and process until very coarsely chopped. Place this mixture in a saucepan with remaining ingredients. Simmer for about 1 hour. Refrigerate until ready to serve.

tartar sauce

Yield: About ⅔ cup

   1 **hard-cooked egg**
   ½ **cup mayonnaise**
   1 **teaspoon prepared mustard**
   ¼ **cup fresh parsley leaves**
   1 **teaspoon chervil**
   1 **teaspoon tarragon**
   ½ **teaspoon sugar**
   2 **teaspoons lemon juice**
   Salt and pepper to taste

Place all ingredients in processor bowl and process with metal blade until parsley is minced. Garnish with chopped chives. Serve with meat, fish, or beef fondue.

grandma lang's cranberry–orange relish

Delicious with chicken or turkey at Thanksgiving! The apple tones down the sharp cranberry–tangerine flavor.

Yield: 2 cups

   ½ **pound cranberries (2 cups)**
   1 **apple, cored, unpeeled, and cut into 6 pieces**
   ½ **tangerine or orange, seeds removed, skin left on, cut into 4 pieces**
   ¾ **cup sugar**

Place cranberries, apple, and tangerine in processor bowl. Process with metal blade until mixture is chopped fine, about 30 seconds. Stop and scrape sides as needed. Add sugar and process until blended. Make 2 or 3 days before needed and refrigerate in a covered jar. Serve cold.

carrot–lemon relish

A tangy relish to serve with poultry.

Yield: 1 cup

   2 **medium carrots, scraped and cut into 1-inch pieces**
   ½ **small lemon, seeded and cut into quarters**
   3 **tablespoons sugar**

Place all ingredients in processor bowl and process with the metal blade until very finely chopped, about 20 seconds. Stop and scrape down sides twice. Store in a covered jar in the refrigerator. Serve cold.

stuffings

basic bread stuffing

The food processor reduces the usual preparation time by about two-thirds.

Yield: Stuffing for an 8- to 12-pound turkey; add 1 cup for each additional pound of bird; halve recipe for a 4-pound chicken.

8 slices stale, but not hard, white or whole-wheat bread, torn in quarters
2 tablespoons fresh parsley leaves
1 medium onion, quartered

2 stalks celery with leaves, cut into 2-inch pieces
1 teaspoon salt
¼ teaspoon freshly ground black pepper
½ cup melted butter or margarine

Process bread, four slices at a time, with the parsley. Turn metal blade on and off quickly just until bread is very coarsely chopped. Empty into a large bowl.

Process onion and celery with the metal blade until coarsely chopped. Add to the bread with the seasonings.

Melt butter and pour over mixture; toss well. Pack loosely into neck and body cavities of poultry. Place any extra stuffing in a pie pan, cover with aluminum foil, and bake 30 to 40 minutes.

Remove stuffing from bird immediately after cooking. Immediately chill that amount not served.

wild-rice and mushroom stuffing

Yield: Stuffing for a 12-pound turkey

2½ cups wild rice
⅓ pound sausage meat
⅓ cup butter or margarine
¾ pound mushrooms, coarsely chopped with the metal blade

2 medium onions, coarsely chopped with the metal blade
1½ teaspoons salt
½ teaspoon freshly ground black pepper

Wash, then cook rice in 5 cups boiling water until tender, about 30 minutes. Drain well.

Brown the sausage meat, add the margarine, mushrooms, and onions. Cook over low heat 3 to 4 minutes. Stir in rice and seasonings. Fill neck and body cavities of the turkey.

stuffing variations

apple stuffing

Add 2 cooking apples, chopped with the metal blade, to the Basic Bread Stuffing.

apricot stuffing

Add 1 cup apricots, coarsely chopped with the metal blade, and ½ cup coarsely chopped nuts to the Basic Bread Stuffing.

brown-rice stuffing

Substitute 4 cups cooked brown rice for bread in the Basic Bread Stuffing.

chestnut stuffing

Add 1 cup boiled, skinned chestnuts, chopped with the metal blade, to the Basic Bread Stuffing.

corn-bread stuffing

Substitute corn bread for white bread in the Basic Bread Stuffing.

date–pumpkin-seed stuffing

Add ½ cup shelled pumpkin seeds and 1 cup dates, coarsely chopped with the metal blade, to the Basic Bread Stuffing.

herb stuffing

Add the following seasonings to the Basic Bread Stuffing: 1 teaspoon thyme or 1 teaspoon sage or 1 teaspoon savory, ½ teaspoon basil, ½ teaspoon thyme, ½ teaspoon marjoram or 2 more tablespoons parsley, 1 teaspoon tarragon, and ½ cup almonds, chopped with the metal blade.

mixed dried-fruit stuffing

Add 1 cup assorted dried fruit, coarsely chopped with the metal blade, and ½ cup chopped nuts to the Basic Bread Stuffing.

mushroom stuffing

Add ½ pound chopped or sliced mushrooms cooked in the butter to the Basic Bread Stuffing.

orange stuffing

Add outer peel of an orange, finely minced with the metal blade, to the Herb Stuffing.

oyster stuffing

Add 1 cup drained, chopped oysters to the Basic Bread Stuffing.

raisin–walnut stuffing

Add 1 cup chopped raisins, ½ cup chopped walnuts, and 1 teaspoon sage to the Basic Bread Stuffing.

water-chestnut–mushroom–nut stuffing

Add 1 8-ounce can drained water chestnuts, halved, and 1 cup chopped almonds to the Mushroom Stuffing.

omelettes

The food processor can be used to shred the cheese and chop or slice many of the ingredients for omelettes.

Crisp ingredients that require softening, such as onions, green peppers, or mushrooms, are chopped or sliced, then cooked in butter in a skillet or omelette pan over low heat. The eggs, lightly mixed with a fork, are added to the skillet.

Ingredients requiring little cooking, such as shredded cheese, chopped tomatoes, or chopped parsley and herbs, are sprinkled over the surface of the eggs.

After a brief stir or two to combine everything, the omelette is stirred no more. The edges of the mixture are lifted as the eggs set on the bottom. This allows the uncooked portions to run underneath. When the eggs are firm the omelette is rolled out of the pan browned side out, onto a heated plate.

Many cooks prefer to prepare 2- or 3-egg omelettes, as these are thinner and more easily handled. If you prepare 5- or 6-egg omelettes, use a 10-inch pan.

parsley and chive omelette

parsley and chive omelette

Yield: 2 servings

½ cup fresh parsley leaves
4 or 5 eggs
¼ teaspoon salt
Pepper to taste
4 blades of chives, cut into ¼-inch
    pieces
1 tablespoon butter
Tomato slices for garnish

Place parsley, eggs, and seasonings in processor bowl. Process with metal blade until parsley is finely chopped. Add chives.

Heat butter in a 10-inch skillet. Pour in the egg mixture. Cook over low heat without stirring. As eggs cook on bottom, lift edges and allow uncooked mixture to run underneath. When all the mixture is set, loosen with a spatula and roll onto a hot dish. Serve at once. Garnish with tomato slices.

bacon and potato omelette

Yield: 3 servings

**3 slices bacon, cut into small
   pieces**
**2 small potatoes, peeled, and
   sliced with the slicing disk**
**8 fresh spinach leaves, stems
   removed, and sliced with the
   slicing disk**
6 eggs, lightly beaten with a fork
Salt and pepper to taste

In a 10-inch skillet, heat bacon briefly. Add potatoes and fry until bacon is crisp and potatoes are lightly browned; add spinach and remove mixture to a small bowl.

Pour eggs, salt, and pepper into skillet. Distribute potato mixture evenly over them. Cook over low heat without stirring. As eggs set on bottom, lift edges and allow uncooked mixture to run underneath. When the omelette is set, fold with a fork and serve immediately.

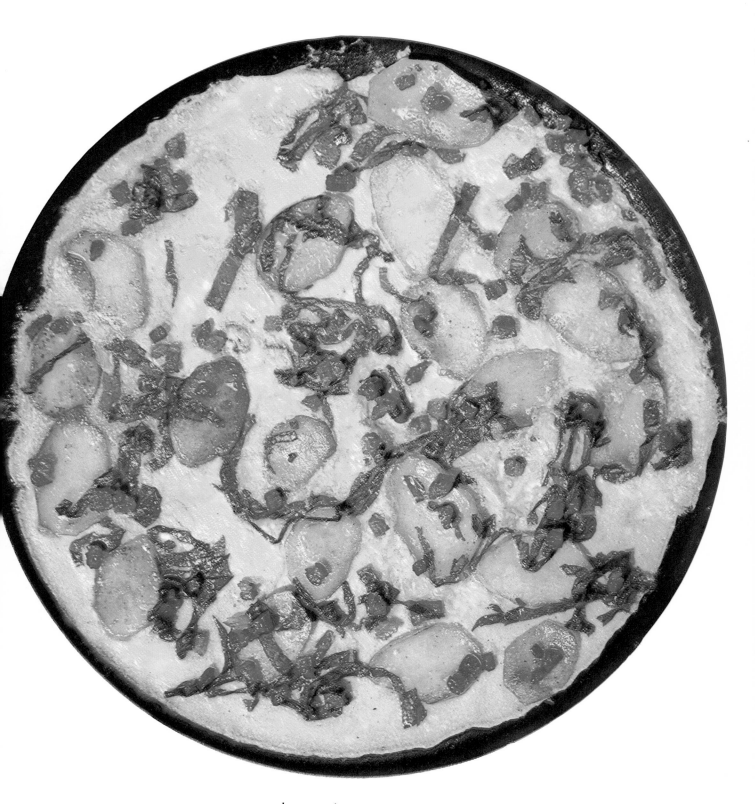

bacon and potato omelette

chinese omelette

Yield: 4 servings

tomato sauce

1 8-ounce can tomato sauce
1 tablespoon olive oil
1 clove garlic
2 tablespoons soy sauce
1 slice fresh gingerroot or ¼ teaspoon ground ginger

omelette

1 small leek, sliced with the slicing disk
2 small onions, sliced with the slicing disk
Several dark-green celery leaves
3 tablespoons vegetable oil
8 eggs, lightly beaten with a fork
4 ounces canned lobster tails, coarsely chopped with the metal blade or by hand
Salt and pepper to taste
½ cup cooked small peas

Simmer together the ingredients for the tomato sauce, about 10 minutes. Remove garlic clove and ginger slice before serving.

Stir-fry the leek, onions, and celery leaves in vegetable oil in a large skillet. Pour in eggs; add lobster, salt, and pepper. Cook over low heat without stirring. As eggs set on bottom, lift edges to allow uncooked mixture to run underneath. When omelette is set, serve at once. Garnish with peas and serve with tomato sauce.

chinese omelette

herb and cheese omelette

Yield: 3 servings

2 tablespoons butter or margarine
1 small pickle, cut into several
    pieces
5 blades chives, cut into 1-inch
    pieces
2 tablespoons fresh dillweed or ½
    tablespoon dried dillweed
6 eggs, lightly beaten with a fork
1 teaspoon savory
6 ounces cheese, grated with the
    shredding disk
Salt and pepper to taste
1 peeled tomato, cut into wedges

Melt butter in a large skillet.

Chop pickle, chives, and dill with metal blade in processor bowl.

Pour eggs into skillet; add chopped ingredients, herbs, cheese, salt, and pepper. Cook over low heat without stirring. When bottom of mixture sets, lift edges and allow uncooked mixture to run underneath. When omelette is completely set, fold and roll out of pan. Garnish with tomato wedges and finely sliced chives.

herb and cheese omelette

crepes

basic crepes

Yield: 20 to 24 crepes

> 1 **cup sifted all-purpose flour**
> 3 **eggs**
> 1½ **cups milk**
> 1 **tablespoon melted butter or**
>   **vegetable oil**
> ⅛ **teaspoon salt**

Place all ingredients in the processor bowl and process with the metal blade until smooth, about 10 seconds. Let the batter stand at room temperature for 1 hour to enable the flour to absorb some of the liquid for ease in handling. Batter may be refrigerated for several hours or overnight.

Place 1 to 1½ tablespoons of the batter in an oiled frypan, preheated to 380° F. Spread the batter quickly into a 6-inch circle with the back of the spoon. Heat until lightly browned, about a minute, and turn with a spatula. Heat about 30 seconds on the other side.

Stack crepes as they are done. Serve at once or refrigerate, tightly wrapped, for 1 or 2 days. They keep frozen up to 2 months.

Fill with your favorite filling and roll. The side cooked first should be on the outside.

cecelia's dessert crepes

Yield: 20 to 24 crepes

> 1 **cup sifted all-purpose flour**
> 3 **eggs**
> 1½ **cups milk**
> 1 **tablespoon melted butter or**
>   **vegetable oil**
> ⅛ **teaspoon salt**
> 2 **tablespoons sugar**
> 1 **tablespoon brandy**

Combine ingredients in processor bowl and proceed as for Basic Crepes.

left: english crepes
right: chocolate crepes

english crepes

Yield: 3 or 4 servings

12 prepared Dessert Crepes
Confectioner's sugar
1 lemon

Fold crepes in quarters. Place 3 or 4 on each plate. Dust with confectioner's sugar. Cut lemon into wedges. Place on crepes. Before eating, squeeze lemon juice over crepes.

left: vanilla fruit crepes
right: crepes a la normandy

vanilla fruit crepes

Yield: 3 or 4 servings

> 8 **ounces cottage cheese**
> 4 **ounces cream cheese, cut into 4**
>   **pieces**
> 1 **teaspoon vanilla**
> ¼ **cup sugar**
> ¼ **to ½ cup fresh fruit**
> 12 **prepared Dessert Crepes**
> 3 **tablespoons strawberry jam**

Place cottage and cream cheeses, vanilla, and sugar in processor bowl. Process with metal blade until smooth. Add fruit and process until coarsely chopped. Cover crepes with the mixture. Fold each in quarters and place 3 or 4 on each plate. Heat jam and dribble over crepes. Serve at once.

chocolate crepes

Yield: 3 or 4 servings

> **12 prepared Dessert Crepes**
> **Chocolate syrup diluted with a**
> **little water**
> **½ cup nuts, chopped with the**
> **metal blade**

Fold crepes in quarters and place 3 or 4 on each plate. Heat chocolate syrup and pour over crepes. Garnish with chopped nuts. These may be served with ice cream.

crepes a la normandy

Yield: 3 or 4 servings

> **4 large apples, peeled, cored, and**
> **coarsely chopped with the**
> **metal blade**
> **3 tablespoons butter or margarine**
> **3 tablespoons apricot brandy**
> **12 prepared Dessert Crepes**
> **Confectioner's sugar**

Cook apple slices in hot butter until tender, 3 or 4 minutes. Add brandy. Distribute mixture over crepes. Roll each. Place 3 or 4 on each plate and dust with confectioner's sugar. Serve at once.

fruit dessert crepes

Yield: 3 or 4 servings

> **½ cup sour cream**
> **2 tablespoons sugar**
> **8 Dessert Crepes**
> **1 10-ounce package frozen,**
> **defrosted blueberries,**
> **strawberries, or raspberries**
> **¼ cup nuts, coarsely chopped**
> **with the metal blade**

Stir together the sour cream and sugar. Place 1 tablespoon down the center of each crepe. Arrange the berries on the sour-cream mixture. Roll up. Top each crepe with a dab of the remaining sour cream and nuts.

asparagus crepes

Yield: 3 or 4 servings

   1 **package frozen asparagus spears,
      cooked according to package
      directions, and drained**
   8 **prepared Basic Crepes**
   4 **or 5 ounces Swiss cheese,
      shredded with the shredding
      disk**
   2 **teaspoons dillweed or 3
      tablespoons chopped fresh
      dillweed**
Salt and pepper to taste
   2 **tomatoes, cut into wedges**

Distribute the asparagus spears over crepes. Sprinkle with shredded cheese and dillweed. Reserve some cheese to use as a garnish. Season with salt and pepper. Roll crepes and place seam side down in a greased baking dish. Add tomato wedges. Sprinkle with reserved cheese. Bake at 400° F for 5 to 10 minutes, until heated through. Serve at once.

salads and dressings

cucumber–radish–sour-cream salad

This is one of my family's favorites. We grow our own cucumbers and radishes and find we have dozens on hand at one time. This recipe helps us use a rather large supply quickly, before they spoil. Home-grown cucumbers do not need to be peeled before using, as they are not coated with wax, as commercially grown ones are, to prevent dehydration.

Yield: 4 to 6 servings

**2 large cucumbers, peeled and cut
    into quarters lengthwise
16 to 24 radishes
½ cup sour cream
Salt to taste**

Slice the cucumbers and radishes with the slicing disk. Remove from processor bowl and combine with sour cream and salt. Serve at once.

peanut–sunflower waldorf salad

Yield: 4 to 6 servings

**4 apples, cored, cut into quarters
2 stalks celery, cut into 3-inch
    pieces
½ cup peanuts
½ cup sunflower seeds
¼ cup raisins
Mayonnaise
Lettuce leaves**

Chop the apples, two at a time, very coarsely with the metal blade. Chop the celery. Chop the peanuts coarsely.

Combine the apples, celery, peanuts, sunflower seeds, and raisins in a large bowl. Add sufficient mayonnaise to moisten. Serve cold in lettuce cups.

cranberry–apple molded salad

Serve this with a chicken or turkey dinner.

Yield: 8 servings

2 cups whole cranberries
½ cup water
1 package cherry-flavored gelatin
1 cup boiling water
1 tablespoon lemon juice
1 unpeeled apple, cored and cut
into 6 pieces
¼ cup walnuts
½ cup mayonnaise

Place cranberries and water in a saucepan. Bring to a boil and simmer 4 to 5 minutes, until tender or until the skins pop. Strain, reserve juice, and set berries aside in a large bowl.

Dissolve gelatin in ½ cup reserved juice. Add boiling water and lemon juice. Chill until the consistency of egg white.

Process apple and walnuts with metal blade until coarsely chopped and add to the cranberries in the large bowl.

Place thickened gelatin and mayonnaise in process bowl and process with metal blade until fluffy. Add this mixture to apples, nuts, and cranberries. Stir until combined, and pour into a 1-quart mold. Chill 4 hours or overnight. Unmold and serve on a bed of lettuce.

vegetable-salad dressing

Yield: About 1½ cups

½ cup sour cream or yogurt
½ cup cottage cheese
½ cucumber, cut into 4 pieces
8 radishes
1 scallion, cut into 1-inch pieces
Salt or seasoned salt to taste
Fresh herbs to taste: dill, parsley,
tarragon, basil, etc.

Place all ingredients in processor bowl and process with metal blade until vegetables are finely chopped. Serve with vegetable salads.

stuffed tomatoes

Yield: 4 servings

4 large ripe tomatoes
1 tablespoon vegetable oil
1 teaspoon vinegar
1 teaspoon Worcestershire sauce
Salt and pepper
1 6½-ounce can tuna, well drained
4 anchovy fillets
2 hard-cooked eggs, quartered

1 teaspoon capers
4 blades of chives, cut into 1-inch
   pieces
2 tablespoons fresh parsley leaves
¼ cup mayonnaise
¾ cup yogurt
1 tablespoon lemon juice
1 teaspoon celery salt

Cut tops off tomatoes and scoop out pulp. Brush insides with a mixture of oil, vinegar, and Worcestershire sauce. Season with salt and pepper. Let stand one hour.

Place remaining ingredients in processor bowl. Process with metal blade, turning on and off quickly 2 or 3 times, just until eggs are coarsely chopped.

Drain Worcestershire sauce mixture from tomatoes and fill with tuna mixture. Place tops on tomatoes. Serve at once.

tossed russian salad with walnut dressing

Yield: 4 servings

salad

1 peeled cucumber, quartered
   lengthwise, and sliced with
   the slicing disk
2 stalks celery, sliced with the
   slicing disk
1 tomato, seeds removed, and
   diced
Salt to taste

dressing

½ cup walnuts
1 clove garlic
Dash cayenne
½ teaspoon ground coriander or 1
   tablespoon fresh coriander
   leaves
1 tablespoon vinegar
3 tablespoons water
½ medium onion
2 tablespoons fresh parsley leaves
Lettuce leaves

Combine salad ingredients. Process walnuts, garlic, and cayenne with metal blade until nuts have formed a paste. Add remaining dressing ingredients and process with metal blade until onion is minced. Pour over salad ingredients and toss lightly. Serve in lettuce cups.

fresh-fruit salads

Use the slicing disk to slice assorted fruits:

Apples
Bananas
Peaches
Pineapple wedges
Strawberries

Arrange on a platter or toss with:

Slivered almonds
Blueberries
Flaked coconut
Pitted dates, halved
Grapes
Salted nuts
Orange segments
Pineapple chunks
Raisins
Raspberries

Sprinkle with pineapple or orange juice and honey, or serve with Low-Calorie Fruit-Salad Dressing.

low-calorie fruit-salad dressing with honey

Yield: 1½ cups

1 cup yogurt
½ cup fresh strawberries or raspberries
1 tablespoon honey (or more, to taste)

Place all ingredients in processor bowl and process with metal blade until strawberries are finely chopped. Serve with fruit salad. Delicious alone as a snack!

deviled eggs

Yield: 8

4 hard-cooked eggs
2 tablespoons mayonnaise
2 tablespoons catsup
2 teaspoons lemon juice
Dash Tabasco sauce
¼ small onion
½ teaspoon mustard
½ teaspoon paprika
Salt and pepper to taste
Chopped chives for garnish

Halve eggs lengthwise. Place yolks, mayonnaise, catsup, lemon juice, Tabasco sauce, onion, and seasonings in processor bowl. Process with metal blade until smooth. Place mixture in a cookie press with a star-shaped tip. Refill egg-white halves. Garnish with chopped chives. Serve at once.

deviled eggs

garlic salad dressing

Yield: About 1 cup

1 cup sour cream
1 clove garlic
2 tablespoons fresh parsley leaves
2 blades chives, cut into 1-inch
pieces
½ teaspoon freshly ground black pepper
Salt to taste

Place all ingredients in processor bowl and process until parsley is minced. Serve with vegetable salads.

fresh-vegetable salads

Select a favorite assortment and toss together or assemble a salad bar with each vegetable in a separate bowl.

Use the slicing disk to slice:

Beets
Red cabbage
White cabbage
Carrots
Cauliflower florets
Celery
Cucumbers
Fresh mushrooms
Olives
Pepperoni for an Italian salad
Radishes
Scallions
Yellow squash
Zucchini (excellent raw)

Use the chopping disk to chop:

Cooked bacon
Cauliflower
Cooked chicken or turkey
Hard-cooked eggs
Green pepper, cut into 8 pieces
Olives
Onions
Parsley

Tomatoes, cut into quarters
Walnuts

Use the shredding disk to grate:

Carrots
Cheese

Add:

Anchovy fillets
Bean sprouts
Capers
Seasoned croutons
Garbanzo beans
Slivers of cooked ham, chicken, or turkey
Red kidney beans
Broken lettuce
Salted nuts
Poppy seeds
Crumbled Roquefort or feta cheese
Slivers of salami or other luncheon meats
Toasted sesame seeds
Sunflower seeds

Serve with your favorite dressing, Garlic Salad Dressing, or Vegetable-Salad Dressing. Many of the Dips (see Contents) may be used as salad dressings.

sandwiches and spreads

The food processor is especially useful for preparing sandwich spreads and sandwich toppings. Use the processor to:
shred lettuce with the slicing disk
grate carrots
slice onions
prepare mayonnaise
prepare herb butters to use in place of
   mayonnaise
slice cucumbers
slice avocados
chop eggs
chop meats
shred cheese

My family particularly appreciates the thin slices of onion and the finely shredded lettuce the processor can prepare as toppings in hoagies, submarines, heroes (depending where you live), and for steak sandwiches. The Herb Butters (see Contents) make interesting substitutes for mayonnaise or butter spreads on the bread.

peanut butter

My children enjoy watching this made!

Yield: About 1 cup

Peanuts (12-ounce bag of raw shelled and blanched peanuts, baked at 350°F for 15 to 20 minutes; or ½ pound very fresh roasted peanuts in the shell, shelled and skinned; or 1 to 2 cups salted peants)
Honey to taste
Salt to taste
Vegetable oil, if needed

Process the peanuts with the metal blade, 1 to 2 cups at a time, until a ball forms on the blades, about 1 to 2 minutes. Commercially made peanut butter usually contains sugar, and you may wish to add about a tablespoon of honey. Process until blended. Taste and add salt to your liking if unsalted peanuts were used.

Occasionally, the peanuts will not form a spread, even after processing for 2 minutes. Correct by dribbling small quantities of vegetable oil in through the tube and processing until a paste is formed.

baked-bean spread

Yield: 1 cup

1 cup baked beans
1 small onion, cut into 6 pieces
1 stalk celery, cut into 2-inch pieces
1 tablespoon lemon juice
¼ teaspoon salt

Combine all ingredients in the processor bowl. Process with the metal blade until ingredients are well blended. Chill and use as a spread for whole-wheat sandwiches. Top the filling with chopped tomatoes, shredded lettuce, and grated cheese. Or, top with crumbled bacon and parsley.

falafel and pita bread

My friends call these Jewish Tacos. They are a traditional Middle Eastern dish becoming extremely popular in this country.

Falafel are made of spiced, crushed chick peas and are served inside Pita bread with lots of lettuce, feta cheese, and a dressing. A good vegetarian dish!

Yield: 4 or 5 servings

4 or 5 Pita Breads (see Index), slit on one side and opened like a pouch

Lettuce, shredded with the slicing disk

Feta cheese, crumbled

Tahini Dressing

falafel

1-pound 4-ounce can chick peas (2 cups cooked), well drained and rinsed with water

2 tablespoons tahini (sesame paste) — optional

1 egg

1 clove garlic

3 tablespoons fresh parsley leaves

1 teaspoon salt

½ teaspoon freshly ground black pepper

¼ teaspoon turmeric

½ teaspoon ground cumin

½ teaspoon baking powder

1 tablespoon olive or sesame oil

Flour for coating

Vegetable oil for deep-frying

Place all the ingredients for the falafel in the processor bowl and process with the metal blade until smooth. Form into 1-inch balls, coat with flour, and deep-fry in vegetable oil at 365°F for about 2 minutes. Remove with a slotted spoon and drain on paper towels.

Falafel may also be prepared by forming the mixture into small patties and frying in a small amount of oil in a skillet. I have also heated the mixture itself in a saucepan to eliminate the need for fat.

Place several falafel in each Pita bread. Top with lettuce, feta cheese, and Tahini Dressing (recipe follows).

tahini dressing for falafel

¼ cup olive or sesame oil

¼ cup water

2 tablespoons lime or lemon juice

1 teaspoon garlic salt

Combine all ingredients and mix well.

mock pizzas

Yield: 8 4-inch pizzas

2 ripe tomatoes, quartered
¼ green pepper, cut into 3 pieces
1 teaspoon oregano
½ teaspoon garlic salt
1 tablespoon olive oil

6 to 8 ounces cheddar cheese,
 shredded with the shredding
 disk
4 English muffins, halved

Place tomatoes, pepper, oregano, garlic salt, and olive oil in processor bowl. Process with metal blade until coarsely chopped. Add cheese and process just until blended. Spread mixture on muffin halves and broil until cheese melts and surface is brown.

chicken-salad spread

Yield: 1¼ cups

1 cup cooked chicken (or more),
 cut into 1-inch cubes
1 stalk celery with leaves, cut into
 1-inch pieces
1 small onion, cut in half
3 tablespoons mayonnaise
Salt to taste

Place all ingredients in food processor bowl and process with metal blade until coarsely chopped. Chop finely for canapés.

chicken-spread variations

Add one or more of these ingredients:

½ cup cooked ham and 2
 teaspoons mustard or
 horseradish
4 slices crisp bacon, broken into
 1-inch pieces
½ cup slivered almonds
½ cup water chestnuts and 1
 tablespoon soy sauce

3 tablespoons fresh parsley leaves
1 tablespoon catsup
4 gherkins, halved
8 small black or green olives
1 small apple, cored and cut into 6
 pieces
½ teaspoon curry powder
1 teaspoon lemon juice

curried turkey spread

Yield: 1½ cups

> 1 cup cooked turkey, cut into
>   1-inch cubes
> 1 stalk celery with leaves, cut into
>   1-inch pieces
> 1 teaspoon lemon juice
> 1 teaspoon curry powder
> ½ teaspoon salt
> ¼ teaspoon freshly ground black
>   pepper
> 1 small apple, cored and cut into 6
>   pieces
> Few slices onion
> 3 to 4 tablespoons mayonnaise

Combine all ingredients in processor bowl and process with the metal blade until coarsely chopped.

ham-salad spread

Yield: About 1¼ cups

> 1 cup cooked ham, cut into 1-inch
>   cubes
> 3 tablespoons mayonnaise
> 1 stalk celery, cut into 1-inch
>   pieces

Place all ingredients in food processor bowl and process with metal blade until coarsely chopped. Chop finely for canapés.

ham-spread variations

Add one or more of the following ingredients:

> 2 hard-cooked eggs, quartered,
>   and ¼ teaspoon garlic powder
> 1 small onion, halved
> 8 small black or green olives
> 4 gherkins, halved, or 2 tablespons
>   relish

> 2 tablespoons orange marmalade
>   and ½ teaspoon prepared
>   mustard
> 2 teaspoons prepared mustard and
>   2 tablespoons fresh parsley
>   leaves

egg-salad spread

Yield: 1½ cups

 6 hard-cooked eggs, cut into
     quarters
 2 stalks celery, cut into 1-inch
     pieces
 ½ teaspoon salt
 ¼ teaspoon freshly ground black
     pepper
 3 tablespoons mayonnaise

Place all ingredients in processor bowl and process with metal blade until coarsely chopped. Process finer if spread is to be used for canapés.

egg-salad spread variations

Add one of these combinations:

 1 tablespoon catsup and 3
     gherkins, halved
 ½ cucumber, peeled and cut into
     1-inch pieces, and 2
     tablespoons fresh parsley
     leaves
 ½ cup cooked chicken and ½
     teaspoon curry powder
 ½ cup cooked chicken and 8 small
     olives
 4 slices crisp bacon, crumbled
 ½ cup cheddar cheese, shredded
     with the shredding disk, and 1
     teaspoon prepared mayonnaise
 ½ green pepper, cut into 1-inch
     pieces, and several slices
     onion

 2 tablespoons chili sauce and
     several slices onion
 4 ounces cooked chicken livers
     and several slices onion
 4 anchovy fillets and 1 teaspoon
     lemon juice
 2 teaspoons lemon juice and 3
     tablespoons fresh parsley
     leaves
 ½ cup ham, cut into 1-inch cubes,
     and 8 small black or green
     olives
 4 anchovy fillets and ½ teaspoon
     paprika
 2 4½-ounce cans deviled ham and
     1 teaspoon prepared mustard

tuna-salad spread

Yield: About 1 cup

    1 6½-ounce can tuna, well drained
    1 stalk celery with leaves, cut into 1-inch pieces
    3 tablespoons mayonnaise

Place in food processor bowl and process with metal blade until coarsely chopped. Process longer if spread is to be used for canapés.

tuna-spread variations

Add one or more of the following ingredients:

  ½ green pepper, cut into 1-inch
      pieces
  2 tablespoons chutney and 1
      hard-cooked egg, quartered
  1 small onion, halved, 2
      hard-cooked eggs, and 1
      teaspoon lemon juice

salmon spread

Yield: About 1¼ cups

    1 7¾-ounce can salmon, drained
    1 stalk celery with leaves, cut into
      1-inch pieces
  ½ green pepper, cut into 1-inch
      cubes
  ¼ cup mayonnaise

Place all ingredients in processor bowl and process with metal blade until coarsely chopped. Process longer if spread is to be used for canapés.

cream-cheese spread

Cream cheese is half fat and should not be used routinely as a substitute for meat or cheese in sandwiches for children unless other good sources of protein are present in the meal.

Yield: 1 cup

¼ cup nuts (or more)
1 8-ounce package cream cheese, cut into 6 pieces

Place nuts and cheese in processor bowl and process with metal blade until nuts are coarsely chopped. Tint cheese with food coloring if spread is to be used for canapés.

cream-cheese spread variations

Add one of the following:

½ cup canned crushed pineapple,
    drained
Omit nuts and add ½ cup olives, a
    few slices onion, and a dash
    Tabasco sauce
2 cups watercress, cut into 1-inch
    pieces

cocktail spread aux fines herbes

This spread is nearly identical in flavor to that of a popular brand name French spread. Try it! It's less expensive when you prepare it yourself.

Yield: About 1 cup

¼ cup cold butter, cut into 3
    pieces
2 small cloves garlic
1 8-ounce package cream cheese,
    cut into 6 pieces
¼ cup fresh parsley leaves
½ teaspoon salt (or more)
Cracked peppercorns (optional)

Process butter and garlic with metal blade until garlic is finely minced, about 30 seconds. Add remaining ingredients, except pepper, and process until parsley is minced.

Shape mixture into a flattened ball. Roll in cracked peppercorns, wrap tightly, and chill for several hours, until firm. Serve with assorted crackers.

soups

indian pea soup

Yield: About 5 cups

1 1-pound can peas, drained,
   liquid reserved
3 cups chicken broth or bouillon
2 teaspoons curry powder
1 teaspoon sugar

¼ cup all-purpose flour shaken in
   a jar with ⅓ cup cold water
   until lump-free
¼ cup slivered almonds
¼ cup raisins
½ cup light cream
Salt and pepper to taste

Place drained peas in processor bowl and process with metal blade until smooth. Place in saucepan with reserved liquid, broth, curry, sugar, and flour mixture. Bring to a boil, stirring constantly. Add almonds and raisins. Simmer 5 minutes. Remove from heat and add cream. Season to taste with salt and pepper. Serve at once.

russian borscht

Yield: 4 cups

- 1 No. 2½ can beets, liquid reserved
- 1 can condensed cream of chicken soup
- 1 clove garlic
- 1 can condensed beef consommé
- ½ teaspoon tarragon
- ½ teaspoon chervil
- ½ teaspoon dried parsley
- Sour cream

Process the beets, cream of chicken soup, and garlic with the metal blade until smooth. Combine with the consommé, herbs, and reserved beet liquid in a 1½-quart container. Chill. Serve cold, garnished with a spoonful of sour cream.

red-bean soup

Yield: 3 cups

- 1 medium onion
- 1 large stalk celery with leaves
- ½ green pepper
- 2 tablespoons vegetable oil
- 1 cup cooked kidney beans
- 1 cup kidney bean liquor
- 1 cup tomato juice
- Thin lemon slice
- Parsley leaves

Chop the onion, celery, and green pepper coarsely with the metal blade. Sauté in the oil until soft. Place sautéed vegetables and beans in the processor bowl and process with the metal blade until smooth, about 15 seconds.

Add mixture to bean liquor and tomato juice in a saucepan and heat thoroughly. Serve hot garnished with a thin slice of lemon and a few parsley leaves.

Picture on opposite page: indian pea soup

avocado soup

Yield: About 4 cups

> **2 ripe, soft avocados, pitted and**
> **   peeled**
> **1 cup chicken broth**
> **1 cup light cream**
> **½ cup yogurt**
> **½ cup dry white wine**
> **1 teaspoon lemon juice**
> **Salt and pepper to taste**

Reserve a few slices of avocado for a garnish and place remaining avocado in processor bowl and process with metal blade until smooth.

Warm broth slightly, add avocado and remaining ingredients. Stir to blend. Serve cold, or heat over moderate heat and serve warm. Garnish with reserved avocado slices.

new england–style clam chowder

Yield: 5 cups

> **2 medium onions, cut into**
> **   quarters**
> **3 tablespoons butter or margarine**
> **2 medium potatoes, peeled and cut**
> **   into several pieces**
> **1 10½-ounce can clams, broth**
> **   reserved**
> **1 cup boiling water and reserved**
> **   clam broth**
> **½ teaspoon salt**
> **⅛ teaspoon pepper**
> **1 tablespoon flour**
> **2 tablespoons cold water**
> **1 pint whole milk**

Chop onions finely with the metal blade and sauté in butter in a large skillet until soft.

Chop potatoes very coarsely with the metal blade and add to the onions in the skillet. Add the boiling water and broth and salt and pepper. Simmer 30 minutes. Add more hot water if necessary.

Combine flour and cold water and stir until smooth. Add to potato–clam mixture and heat until thickened. Add milk and heat through. Serve at once with chowder crackers.

Picture on opposite page: avocado soup

cream of mushroom soup

Yield: 4 servings

1 small onion, quartered
1 stalk celery, cut into 3-inch pieces
4 to 6 tablespoons butter or margarine

1 pound fresh mushrooms
3½ cups whole milk
¼ cup all-purpose flour
Salt
Fresh parsley sprigs

Chop onion and celery coarsely with metal blade. Cook over low heat in butter in a large skillet until soft.

Slice the mushrooms into "T" shapes with the slicing disk (by wedging them into the tube sideways) and add to onions and celery. Cook 2 to 3 minutes. Add 3 cups of the milk to the mushrooms in the skillet.

Shake ½ cup cold milk in a jar with the flour until no lumps are present. Add to the skillet. Heat and stir over moderate heat until soup is thickened and begins to boil. Salt to taste. Serve at once garnished with parsley sprigs.

vichyssoise

Yield: 6 cups

4 medium potatoes, peeled and cut into 1-inch cubes
3½ cups boiling water
5 chicken bouillon cubes
3 tablespoons butter
1½ cups onion or leeks, chopped with the metal blade
1 cup heavy cream
1 cup milk
1 teaspoon salt
¼ teaspoon pepper
Minced chives
Paprika

Combine potatoes, water, bouillon, butter, and onion. Cover and cook until the potatoes are very tender, about 30 minutes. Drain, reserving liquid.

Process the drained vegetables, ½ at a time, with the metal blade until they are very smooth. Return vegetables to their cooking liquid. Add cream, milk, salt, and pepper. Chill thoroughly. Serve cold garnished with minced chives and paprika. (Soup may also be reheated and served hot.)

swiss fondue soup

swiss fondue soup

This soup is thickened with bread crumbs and laced with shredded cheese and wine.

Yield: 4 to 6 servings

> 8 dry, white bread slices, each torn
>   in quarters
> ½ pound Swiss cheese, shredded
>   with shredding disk
> 3 cups hot chicken broth
> 1 cup dry white wine
> 10 blades of chives, sliced fine
> 1 teaspoon fresh parsley leaves or
>   dillweed, chopped
> Salt and pepper to taste

garnish

> 1 small onion, sliced with the slicing disk
> 4 slices bacon, halved

Process bread with the metal blade, four slices at a time, until coarsely chopped. Add bread and cheese to hot broth. Let stand 10 minutes. Process half at a time in processor bowl with the metal blade until smooth. Place in a saucepan and bring to a boil. Add wine, chives, and parsley. Season to taste with salt and pepper. Keep warm.

In a skillet, brown onion rings and bacon until onion is glazed. Serve soup at once, garnished with bacon and onion.

hearty lentil soup

Lentils, unlike other dried beans, do not have to be soaked prior to cooking.

Yield: 5 to 6 cups

1½ cups lentils
1 medium onion, quartered, and
chopped with the metal blade
2 large stalks celery with leaves,
cut into 3-inch sections, and
chopped with the metal blade
4 cups water
⅓ pound smoked pork neck bones
with meat attached
Salt and pepper

Place beans, onion, celery, and water in saucepan with neck bones. Simmer 45 to 60 minutes or until beans are tender. Remove bones and trim off meat.

Process soup 1 to 2 cups at a time with the metal blade until smooth. Add meat and rewarm if necessary. Season to taste. Serve hot.

french onion soup

Yield: 5 to 6 cups

3 tablespoons vegetable oil
3 cups onions, quartered, and
coarsely chopped a few at a
time with metal blade
4 cups rich beef stock
½ cup vermouth
Slices of dry French bread
Swiss cheese, grated with
shredding disk
Grated Parmesan cheese

Place oil and onions in a frying pan; cover, and cook over low heat until soft, about 10 minutes. Remove lid, turn up heat and brown onions until they are a rich, mahogony brown, about 10 minutes or longer. Stir every 2 to 3 minutes and do not burn. Add stock and simmer 1 hour. Stir in vermouth.

Place soup in bowls. Add a slice of dry French bread to each and sprinkle with a mixture of Swiss and Parmesan cheeses. Place bowls in a hot oven or under broiler until cheese melts. Serve immediately.

gazpacho

There are countless variations to this flavorful cold soup. You can adjust the ingredients according to vegetables available or in season. Those given here are a suggested assortment. Herbs and parsley also may be added.

Yield: About 4 to 5 cups

Chop each of these vegetables separately until coarse in the processor bowl, with the metal blade. Remove to a large jar.

**1 medium onion, peeled and
  quartered
1 clove garlic
2 green peppers, seeded and
  quartered
4 tomatoes, peeled, seeds removed
  if you wish, quartered
1 cucumber, peeled and cut into 6
  pieces**

Add and chill well:

**Salt and pepper to taste
⅓ cup olive oil
¼ cup lemon juice
2 or more cups tomato juice
1 tablespoon dry sherry**

Serve cold with a dollop of sour cream on top.

nut breads and quick breads

nut breads

Be sure to use your food processor to prepare several of the nut breads. What a delight it is to use. The entire loaf can be mixed, fruits cut up, nuts chopped, all in the processor bowl with only a few utensils to clean up. Take care not to overprocess once the nuts have been added or they will lose their identity and will not be the crunchy ingredient they are meant to be. Overprocessing also overdevelops the gluten in the flour and will cause the breads to be less delicate in texture.

quick breads — pancakes muffins, and waffles

Most quick breads are prepared by combining the liquid ingredients and melted fat or oil and stirring them all at once, but briefly, into the combined dry ingredients.

This same technique is used with the food processor. Liquids and any ingredients to be chopped are processed with the metal blade. This mixture is poured into a bowl containing the combined dry ingredients. Stirring is done by hand only to moisten dry ingredients. The baking powder always must be thoroughly distributed throughout the flour, because stirring is minimal after liquids are added.

Do not use the processor for the final mixing, as it tends to overprocess muffin, pancake, and waffle batters. The product then has a tendency to be tough, heavy, and coarse.

cream puffs and popovers

The processor will quickly combine the ingredients for these and eliminate the usual tedious stirring necessary for cream puffs.

what type of flour should be used in quick breads?

Whole-wheat flour is more nutritious than enriched white flour and has been used in these recipes wherever possible. However, it is not suited for use in many products, because it will produce a heavy, compact baked product. Flours are discussed further in the introductory section for yeast breads.

popovers

Hollow, mushroom shapes to be served piping hot with butter.

Yield: 8 or 9

- **1 cup sifted all-purpose flour**
- **½ teaspoon salt**
- **1 tablespoon vegetable oil**
- **2 eggs**
- **1 cup milk**

Place all ingredients in the processor bowl and process with the metal blade until smooth, about 10 seconds.

Lightly grease muffin pans or custard cups. Fill cups ½ full with the batter. Bake at 450° F for 15 minutes; reduce heat to 325° F and bake another 30 minutes. Serve at once.

apple–raisin bread

Yield: 1 9 × 5-inch loaf

¾ cup brown sugar
½ cup cold butter or margarine, cut into 6 pieces
2 eggs
1 teaspoon cinnamon
¼ teaspoon cloves
½ teaspoon salt

2 large apples, peeled, cored, and each cut into 8 pieces
½ cup raisins
2 cups sifted all-purpose flour
¼ teaspoon baking soda
2 teaspoons baking powder
½ cup walnuts (optional)

Place sugar, butter, eggs, spices, and salt in the processor bowl. Process with the metal blade until light, about 15 seconds. Add apples and process until finely chopped. Add raisins; process 2 seconds.

Stir together the flour, soda, and baking powder. Add to the processor bowl. Turn blade on and off quickly 4 or 5 times, until flour is blended in. Do not overprocess.

Pour into a 9 × 5-inch loaf pan and bake at 350°F for 55 to 60 minutes. Cool on a wire rack. If you like nuts, ½ cup walnuts may be added with the flour.

banana–orange nut bread

Yield: 1 9 × 5-inch loaf

1 cup sugar
½ cup hydrogenated shortening
2 eggs
½ teaspoon salt
Skin of ½ tangerine or peeled outer rind of 1 small orange

2 bananas, each broken into 8 pieces
½ cup walnuts
2 cups sifted all-purpose flour
1½ teaspoons baking powder
½ teaspoon baking soda

Insert metal blade in processor bowl. Add sugar, shortening, eggs, salt, and rind. Process until light and the rind is finely chopped, about 15 seconds. Add bananas; process 4 or 5 seconds. Scrape down sides and break up any remaining large pieces. Add walnuts, process 1 second.

Stir together the flour, baking powder, and soda. Add to the bowl and process by turning on and off quickly 4 or 5 times or just until blended. Do not overprocess.

Pour into a greased 9 × 5-inch loaf pan and bake at 350°F for 55 to 60 minutes. Cool on a rack and serve warm. Top with a little whipped cream or cream cheese if you are not too concerned with calories.

date–nut–carrot whole-wheat bread

A rich cake chock-full of good things!

Yield: 1 9 × 5-inch loaf

2 medium carrots, cleaned and
   scraped
¾ cup brown sugar
½ cup cold butter or margarine,
   cut into 6 pieces
2 eggs
½ teaspoon salt

¼ cup orange juice
½ cup pitted dates, halved
¾ cup flaked coconut (optional)
½ cup walnuts
1 cup sifted all-purpose flour
1 cup whole-wheat flour
2 teaspoons baking powder
¼ teaspoon baking soda

Grate the carrots with the shredding disk. Remove from the bowl and set aside. Insert the metal blade in the food processor bowl. Add the sugar, butter, eggs, and salt. Process until light, about 15 seconds. Add orange juice. Process until it is combined. Add grated carrots, dates, coconut, and walnuts. Process by turning on and off quickly 3 or 4 times. Scrape down sides twice.

Stir together the flour, baking powder, and soda. Add to the bowl. Process by turning blade on and off quickly 4 or 5 times, until ingredients are combined. Do not overprocess, or cake will be tough and nuts and fruits pulverized.

Pour into a greased 9 × 5-inch loaf pan and bake at 350°F for about 55 minutes. Remove from pan and cool on a wire rack. Slice when completely cool.

fruit muffins

Yield: 12

1 cup milk
1 egg
2 tablespoons vegetable oil
2 tablespoons sugar
1 teaspoon salt

About 1 cup dates, apples, or
   bananas cut into 1-inch pieces,
   or blueberries
2 cups sifted all-purpose flour
3 teaspoons baking powder

Place milk, egg, oil, sugar, salt, and the desired fruit in the processor bowl. Process with the metal blade until the fruit is coarsely chopped.

Sift together in a large mixing bowl the flour and baking powder. Pour in the liquid–fruit mixture and stir just until the dry ingredients are moistened.

Fill greased muffin pans ⅔ full. Bake at 425°F for 15 to 20 minutes. Remove from pan at once and serve hot with butter.

cheese muffins

Follow directions for Fruit Muffins, but substitute 1 cup grated cheese, grated with the shredding disk, for the fruit.

wheat-germ muffins

Using Fruit Muffins recipe, substitute 1 cup wheat germ for 1 cup of the all-purpose flour.

whole-wheat muffins

Use the Fruit Muffins recipe, but substitute 1 cup whole-wheat flour for 1 cup of the all-purpose flour.

cream-puff shells

Yield: 8 to 12 large puffs
24 to 36 small puffs

1 cup water	1 cup sifted all-purpose
½ cup butter or margarine	flour
¼ teaspoon salt	4 eggs

Place the water, butter, and salt in a saucepan. Heat to boiling but do not evaporate. Add the flour all at once and stir vigorously. Cook, stirring continuously, until the mixture forms a ball and no longer clings to the sides of the pan, about 1 to 2 minutes. Remove from heat and let stand for 5 minutes.

Insert metal blade in processor bowl. Add the batter and process 15 seconds. Add the eggs and process until dough is smooth and shiny, about 30 seconds.

Drop the mixture from a teaspoon or tablespoon, depending on size desired, onto a greased baking sheet. Or press through the star-shaped tip of a cookie press. Leave 2 inches between each to allow for spreading.

Bake in a preheated 450°F oven for 15 minutes. Reduce the heat to 325°F and continue baking 25 minutes longer. Remove from baking sheet with a spatula and cool on a wire rack.

Shortly before serving time, cut off the tops and fill with pudding, whipped cream, berries, or other desired dessert filling. Or, fill with tuna or chicken salads and serve as a main dish or the small ones as appetizers. Serve at once after filling.

yeast breads

One of the greatest pleasures for me and my family during the writing of this book was the development of the recipes for yeast breads. Like most people, we enjoy having the aroma of baking bread permeate our home. The flavor of freshly baked breads and rolls is heavenly. By the time commercially baked bread is prepared, delivered to the store, and purchased, its rich, buttery, fresh-baked flavor is lost.

Your food processor can handle enough dough to make one 8½ × 4½-inch loaf or a 9 × 5-inch loaf if additional ingredients are used — an ample loaf for 4 to 6 people to devour at one meal!

Several changes in standard bread-making techniques were necessary, because the processor cannot knead large quantities of heavy doughs. If you are an experienced baker, some of these changes will be apparent in the recipes. Also, most food processors are purchased as time- and labor-saving appliances for the working homemaker, and the recipes here were created with this in mind.

You'll find the time required to prepare yeast breads, from start to eating, has been reduced to about two hours. Kneading time is only one or two minutes, rather than the usual ten minutes. To cut down on messy cleanup chores, only the processor bowl and a few measuring utensils are used for preparation.

Even if you have never made bread before, you should find these recipes easy to follow.

which type of flour is best to use in breads?

The most nutritious flour is one prepared from the whole grain. Nearly all the nutrients present in the original grain remain in the milled flour. In enriched flours the bran layer and germ, the most nutritious portions of the kernel, are sifted out and removed from the milled flour. This is done to increase the keeping quality of the flour.

Whole-grain flours require refrigeration if not used within a few weeks. The presence of the oils in the germ tends to cause rancidity. Both the germ and bran act to reduce the volume of loaves and cause them to be rather compact. The bran shears the gluten in the dough and the germ tends to soften it. Gluten is the rubbery protein portion of the flour that is developed by kneading. It traps carbon dioxide gas bubbles released by yeast and coagulates during baking to form the sponge-like structure responsible for bread's shape and form. If this structure is softened, sheared, or weakened, a compact loaf results.

Refined, enriched flour produces light loaves, but only thiamine, riboflavin, niacin, and iron are added back to the flour after milling; other lost minerals, vitamins, and fiber are not.

The best solution seems to be to use half whole-grain flour and half enriched flour in recipes for breads if good volume is important to you. Loaves will have some of the nutrients and fiber from the whole grain and be reasonably light in texture.

For sweet breads and rolls, only enriched flour should be used or the results will be disappointing — heavy, non-delicate, coarse products. Use raisins, dried fruits, or nuts to increase nutritional values.

how should flour be measured?

In these recipes for yeast breads, stir the specified flour in the bag and spoon it gently into the measuring cups. Level with the straight edge of a spatula. Never sift whole-grain flours. The bran and germ clog the sifter!

which type of yeast is best, active dry or cake?

Cake yeast is packaged in foil and must be kept refrigerated and used within a few weeks. The yeast cells are live and merely need to be dispersed in any lukewarm liquid before using in doughs. Either warm water or milk at about 85 to 95°F will do.

Active dry yeast can be stored at room temperature for many months because the yeast cells have been inactivated by drying. The water must be restored to the cells by soaking the yeast in lukewarm water at 105 to 115°F before using. Hottest tap water is usually about 130°F — much too hot! Soaking should not be done in milk or the cells will not rehydrate properly. Check water temperature with a thermometer. It the water is too cool, cells will not rehydrate properly; if too hot, you will kill the yeast and have a non-leavened loaf.

Active dry yeast has been selected for use in these recipes. If it is rehydrated properly in water at the correct temperature, its action is identical to that of cake yeast; and dry yeast is more conveniently stored.

how is yeast handled?

Yeast is a one-celled plant that lives on sugars added to the dough or formed from the starch in flour. It grows rapidly in a warm location but will be destroyed if the temperature reaches 130°F during the rehydration of yeast or the rising of the dough.

which liquid should be used, water or milk?

Many yeast-bread recipes specify the use of milk because it adds nutrients to the loaf. If milk is used as the liquid ingredient, it must be scalded to destroy enzymes and bacteria present. These would interfere with the growth of yeast. The milk is then cooled to lukewarm before being added to the dough, so that it will not inactivate the yeast cells.

As a time-saving measure, lukewarm water has been recommended in all the recipes given here. If you wish to use milk, rehydrate the yeast in about ¼ cup of lukewarm water (necessary for active dry yeast) and add scalded, lukewarm milk in place of the remaining water called for in the recipe.

how are mixing and kneading done in the food processor?

Mixing and kneading are necessary to distribute ingredients, but mainly to develop the gluten in the flour. You'll note in these recipes about half of the flour is processed with the sugar, oil, and liquid ingredients. The processor motor can easily handle this batter and

develops the gluten in this portion of the flour rapidly.

After a brief rising period, the remaining half of the flour is added and processed until a ball of dough forms on the blades or until the motor begins to stall.

Some doughs are very sticky and the blades become enmeshed and the motor begins to struggle. Should this occur, stop the processor at that point and remove the dough.

In either case, processing will not be adequate to develop all the gluten in this second portion of flour sufficiently. A brief period of hand kneading on a floured board is recommended for optimum loaf volume.

what are the best conditions for rising of the dough?

Two rising periods are necessary for yeast breads. In these recipes, the first follows the processing of the first half of the flour with yeast and the liquid ingredients. During this period, the yeast begins to multiply rapidly throughout the dough so ample numbers of cells will be available during the second rising and produce sufficient carbon dioxide to leaven the shaped loaf. Many by-products are produced during these growth and multiplication periods, and these give yeast breads their characteristic flavor.

In the recipes given here, the first rising can be done directly in the food processor bowl with about half the flour and all the sugar and water present. Leave the lid on the bowl and the pusher in the tube to retain maximum warmth and moisture. If eggs are used, bring them to room temperature first by letting them sit in warm water so they will not chill the dough and slow the rate of yeast growth.

The second rising after shaping can be done in a barely warm oven, one about the temperature of a hot summer day, about 80 to 85°F. At this temperature the maximum amount of flavor substances will be produced without the development of sour flavors in the loaf.

To achieve this temperature range, place the shaped loaf in a cool oven with a pan of boiling water beneath. Warm an electric oven by turning it on for only 10 to 15 seconds. Place dough in a gas oven warmed by its pilot light. Remember, temperatures of 130°F during rising will kill the yeast, and no rising will take place!

which types of pans should be used?

The processor will handle successfully only about three cups of dough. Each recipe yields this amount, and an 8 × 4-inch or 8½ × 4½-inch loaf pan will give the best loaf shape. Smaller pans will cause the loaf top to mushroom.

You may use glass pans, but remember to reduce the baking temperature by 25°F, or the loaf sides and bottom will become too brown and dry. Glass absorbs too much heat!

If aluminum pans are used, they should be dull or frosted. Shiny pans reflect heat and prevent the bottom and sides from browning.

where should the loaf be placed in the oven?

Place loaves and rolls on the center shelf, so the bottoms and tops are evenly done.

final tips about baking

The final loaf volume is always about three times the volume of the original dough. Fill pans only half full. After doubling during the second rising, the dough volume increases again by 50 percent during the early stages of baking.

Cool the loaves and rolls on a wire rack to prevent condensation of steam. Eat at once!

points to remember

Excessive rising will produce a sour loaf with large holes. Insufficient rising produces a compact loaf with little flavor. Sufficient kneading or manipulation of the dough is necessary to develop the gluten in flour. Underdeveloped gluten will not trap leavening gases well and will result in a compact loaf.

For a shiny crust: Brush with a little egg and water before baking.

For a soft crust: Brush with melted shortening before baking.

For a crisp crust: Brush with water before baking and twice during baking.

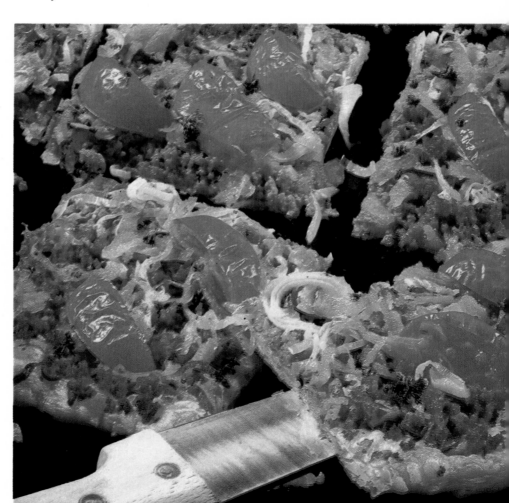

pizza with ground beef, parsley, sliced onion, and tomato wedges

110

light rye bread

light rye bread

Yield: 1 loaf

1 package active dry yeast
¾ cup lukewarm water
　(105–115° F)
1 tablespoon sugar
1 teaspoon salt
2 tablespoons vegetable oil
1¼ cups all-purpose flour
1¼ cups rye flour
1 tablespoon caraway seeds
　(optional)
1 egg, lightly beaten

Dissolve yeast in the lukewarm water in the processor bowl. Add sugar, salt, oil, and the all-purpose flour. Process with the metal blade for 15 seconds. Let rise in the processor bowl for 20 to 30 minutes. Add the rye flour and caraway seeds. Process until a ball forms on the blades, about 5 seconds.

Knead dough on a lightly floured surface for 1 to 2 minutes, until smooth and elastic. Form into a loaf about 8 inches long, with tapered ends, and place on a greased baking sheet. Cover and let rise in a warm place (80–85° F) until doubled in bulk, about 45 to 60 minutes.

Brush crust with lightly beaten egg and sprinkle with additional caraway seeds. Bake in a preheated 375° F oven for 30 to 40 minutes. Cool on a wire rack. Serve at once. Loaf is compact, moist, and so good!

white bread

Yield: 1 loaf

  ¾ cup lukewarm water
     (105–115°F)
  1 package active dry yeast
  2 tablespoons sugar
  ½ teaspoon salt
  2 tablespoons vegetable oil
  2½ cups all-purpose flour

Place water in the food processor bowl, add yeast and allow it to dissolve. Add sugar, salt, oil, and 1½ cups of the flour. Process with the metal blade for 15 seconds. Let rise in the processor bowl for 20 to 30 minutes. Add the remaining 1 cup of flour. Process only until a ball of dough forms on the blades.

Remove and knead dough on a floured surface for 1 to 2 minutes, until smooth and elastic. Shape into a loaf and press into a well-greased 8 × 4-inch loaf pan. Cover and rise in a warm (80–85°F) place for 30 to 45 minutes, until doubled in bulk.

Place in a preheated 375°F oven and bake for 30 minutes. Remove from pan immediately and cool on a wire rack. Serve at once.

dark german rye bread

Very dark in color, sweet, and moist.

Yield: 1 loaf

  1 package active dry yeast
  ¾ cup lukewarm water (105–115°F)
  3 tablespoons molasses
  1 tablespoon cocoa
  1 teaspoon salt
  2 tablespoons vegetable oil
  1¼ cups all-purpose flour
  1¼ cups rye flour
  1 tablespoon caraway seeds
  1 egg, lightly beaten

Dissolve yeast in lukewarm water in the processor bowl. Add molasses, cocoa, salt, oil, and the all-purpose flour. Process with the metal blade for 15 seconds. Let rise in the food processor bowl for 20 to 30 minutes. Add rye flour and caraway seeds. Process until a ball forms on the blades, about 5 seconds, or until motor begins to stall.

Remove dough and knead on a floured surface 1 to 2 minutes, until smooth. Shape into an 8-inch oblong loaf. Place on a greased baking sheet. Cover and let rise in a warm (80–85°F) place about 45 minutes or until doubled in bulk.

Brush with highly beaten egg and sprinkle with additional caraway seeds. Bake in a preheated 375°F oven for 30 to 40 minutes. Cool on a wire rack. Slice and serve at once.

dill–onion bread

dill–onion bread

Yield: 1 loaf

Follow recipe for Light Rye Bread, but add 2 medium onions, cut into quarters, and 1 egg at room temperature with the first addition of flour. Add 1 tablespoon dillseeds with the second addition of flour.

cottage-cheese–dill bread

Yield: 1 loaf

1 package active dry yeast	1 small onion, peeled and
¼ cup lukewarm water	quartered
(105–115° F)	1 cup creamed cottage cheese,
1 tablespoon sugar	warmed to lukewarm so it will
2 tablespoons vegetable oil	not delay rising
1 egg, room temperature	2½ cups all-purpose flour
1 teaspoon salt	1 tablespoon dillseeds

Dissolve yeast in warm water in the processor bowl. Add sugar, oil, egg, salt, onion, and cheese. Process with the metal blade for 15 seconds or until the onion is finely minced. Add 1¼ cups of the flour and process until smooth, about 15 seconds. Let rise in processor bowl 20 to 30 minutes. Add remaining flour and dillseeds. Process until a ball forms on the blades or the motor begins to stall, about 5 seconds.

Knead on a floured surface 1 to 2 minutes, until smooth. Pat dough into a well-greased 8½ × 4½-inch loaf pan. Cover and let rise in a warm (80–85° F) place, about 45 minutes or until doubled in bulk.

Bake at 375° F for 30 to 35 minutes. Cool loaf on a wire rack and serve warm.

french bread

french bread

The shaped loaf is brushed with water and baked in a steamy oven to form a crisp, crunchy crust. Serve this with a bottle of wine and an assortment of your favorite cheeses for Saturday's lunch.

Yield: 1 loaf

1 **package active dry yeast**	2 **tablespoons vegetable oil**
1 **scant cup lukewarm water**	1¼ **teaspoons salt**
(110–115° F)	3 **cups all-purpose flour**

Dissolve yeast in lukewarm water in the processor bowl. Add oil, salt, and 1½ cups of the flour. Process with the metal blade about 15 seconds. Let dough rise in the covered processor bowl for about 30 minutes. Add remaining flour and process until a ball forms or the blades slow down and the motor begins to stall.

Remove dough and knead on a floured board for about 2 minutes. Shape dough into a long roll about 2 inches in diameter. Place on a greased baking sheet, cover with a damp towel, and let it rise in a warm place (80–85° F) until doubled in bulk, about 45 minutes.

Slash the top of the loaf with a sharp knife diagonally ⅛ to ¼-inch deep every 1½ inches. Brush the loaf with cold water and place on the top oven shelf. On the second shelf beneath the loaf, place 1 cup of boiling water in a cake pan. Turn the oven on to 400° F and bake loaf 30 to 40 minutes.

After 10 minutes of baking, brush or spray loaf with cold water. Repeat again in 15 minutes. Cool loaf on a rack and serve at once.

114

pita bread

A traditional Middle Eastern flat bread served split and filled as a sandwich or quartered and served with dips.

Yield: 8 pitas, 5 inches each

1 package active dry yeast
1 cup lukewarm water (105–115° F)
1 tablespoon sugar
3 cups all-purpose flour
1½ teaspoons salt

Dissolve yeast in the warm water in the processor bowl. Add sugar and 2 cups of flour. Process with the metal blade for 15 seconds. Let rise in processor bowl 30 minutes. Add remaining flour and salt. Process until ball forms on blades.

Remove and knead on a floured board about 2 minutes. Cut dough into 8 pieces and form each into a round ball. Let stand covered with a towel for 10 minutes.

On a lightly floured surface flatten each ball with the heel of the hand. Roll to form a 4- to 5-inch round. Do not crease or poke dough, or pita will not separate properly after baking.

Place on a lightly greased baking sheet and bake immediately in a preheated 450° F oven on the top oven shelf for 8 to 10 minutes. Prepare and bake the first four. Then prepare the second four.

Rounds should not be allowed to rise before baking. If they do, reflatten by patting. Serve pita warm.

For sandwiches, split one side, open to form a pocket, and fill with Falafel, lettuce, cheese, salad dressing, or your own favorite filling.

If the Pita breads become too dry before they have adequately browned, reduce the baking time and brown the tops under the broiler.

salt sticks

Yield: 12 rolls

1 recipe White Bread
Caraway seeds
Kosher (coarse) salt

1 egg beaten with 1 tablespoon
water

Prepare yeast dough and knead as directed. Roll dough into a 12-inch circle and cut with a sharp knife or pizza cutter into 12 pie-shaped wedges. Begin with the wide end and roll each wedge tightly. Moisten the point and seal to the roll. Curve each roll to form a crescent and place on a greased baking sheet. Let rise in a warm (80–85° F) place until doubled in bulk.

Brush each roll with the egg mixture, sprinkle with caraway seeds and a little salt. Bake in a preheated 400° F oven for 12 to 15 minutes. Serve at once.

brioche rolls

Rich, golden, French rolls with a topknot. In France these delicate rolls are most often served at breakfast.

Yield: 8 to 10

1 package active dry yeast	2 eggs, room temperature
¼ cup lukewarm water (105–115° F)	2½ cups all-purpose flour
¼ cup sugar	½ cup cold butter, cut into 6 pieces
½ teaspoon salt	

Dissolve yeast in lukewarm water in the processor bowl. Add 1 tablespoon of the sugar, salt, eggs, and 1¼ cups flour. Process 20 seconds. Let rise in processor bowl for 20 to 30 minutes. Add butter and remaining sugar. Process until blended, about 15 seconds. Add remaining 1¼ cups of flour and process until a ball forms on the blades or motor begins to stall.

Knead lightly 1 to 2 minutes. Set aside ¼ of the dough. Cut the remaining ¾ into 8 or 10 pieces. Roll each into a smooth ball and place in greased muffin tins or fluted brioche-tart molds, if you have them.

Cut reserved dough into 8 or 10 pieces; roll in balls. Make an indentation in the center of each large ball. Moisten, and press the small ball into the dent. Let rise in a warm (80–85° F) place for 30 to 45 minutes, until doubled in bulk. Brush each brioche with beaten egg.

Bake at 375° F for about 15 to 20 minutes. Serve warm with sweet butter or marmalade.

sweet-roll dough

Yield: see following recipes

> 1 package active dry yeast
> ½ cup lukewarm water
> (105–115° F)
> ¼ cup sugar
> ½ teaspoon salt
> ¼ cup butter or margarine, cut
> into 4 pieces
> 1 egg, room temperature
> 2½ cups all-purpose flour

Dissolve yeast in warm water in the processor bowl. Add sugar, salt, butter, egg, and 1½ cups flour. Process 15 seconds. Let rise in the processor bowl for 20 minutes. Add remaining cup of flour and process until a ball forms on the blades, about 5 seconds.

Remove dough and knead on a floured surface for 1 to 2 minutes. Shape, rise, and bake as directed in the following recipes.

Rising time for sweet-roll dough is longer than for bread dough because sugar slows the growth of the yeast.

rum–raisin bread

Yield: 1 loaf

> 1 recipe Sweet-Roll Dough
> ¾ cup raisins soaked for 15 to 20
> minutes in 2 or 3 tablespoons
> rum
> 1½ teaspoons cinnamon
> 3 tablespoons sugar
> Confectioner's Icing (optional)

Prepare recipe for Sweet-Roll Dough as directed, but add rum–raisin mixture just prior to the second addition of flour.

Roll out dough to an 8 × 15-inch rectangle, dampen the surface with a little water, and sprinkle with the cinnamon–sugar mixture. Beginning with the short end, roll dough tightly; seal ends. Place seam end down in an 8 × 4-inch loaf pan. Cover and let rise in a warm place for 45 to 60 minutes.

Bake in a preheated 375° F oven for about 30 minutes. Cool loaf on a wire rack. Ice, if you wish, with Confectioner's Icing.

soft pretzels

These pretzels are like those you can buy from pretzel stands on city street corners in many cities.

soft pretzels

Yield: 8 to 10 soft pretzels

   1 **package active dry yeast**
   ⅔ **cup lukewarm water
        (105–115° F)**
   1 **tablespoon vegetable oil**
   2 **tablespoons sugar**
   ½ **teaspoon salt**
   1 **egg, lightly beaten and divided
        in half**
   2¼ **cups all-purpose flour**
   1½ **teaspoons lye (handle with
        care!) dissolved in 2 cups cold
        water in a stainless-steel pan
        (This very dilute mixture of
        lye is harmless and gives
        pretzels their characteristic
        flavor.)
            or**
   2 **teaspoons baking soda dissolved
        in 2 cups water may be used in
        place of the lye mixture.
        (Flavor is similar to, but not
        the same as, the dilute lye
        solution.)**
   Kosher (coarse) salt
   1 **tablespoon cold water**

Dissolve the yeast in the warm water in the processor bowl. Add the oil, sugar, plain salt, ½ the beaten egg, and 1¼ cups flour. Process with the metal blade for 20 seconds and let rise in the processor bowl for 30 minutes. Add remaining flour and process until a ball forms on the blades.

Knead the dough on a lightly floured surface for 1 to 2 minutes. Cut the dough into 8 or 10 pieces. Roll each piece into a 16-inch long rope. Dip into the lye or baking-soda solution. Form into a pretzel. Seal ends well. Place on a lightly greased baking sheet. Let rise slightly, but not until doubled in bulk or the texture will be spongy rather than crisp (about 15 minutes).

Combine remaining ½ egg with 1 tablespoon cold water and brush the pretzels with the mixture. Sprinkle with coarse salt.

Bake in a preheated 400° F oven for about 15 minutes. Cool on a wire rack. Serve warm.

bugnes

bugnes

Bugnes (pronounced buns) are sweet fritters with an unusual shape.

Yield: About 50

1 recipe Sweet-Roll Dough
Vegetable oil for deep-fat frying
1 cup confectioner's sugar
1 teaspoon cinnamon
1 teaspoon nutmeg

Prepare Sweet-Roll Dough as recipe directs. Roll out dough to 1/16-inch thickness on a floured surface. Cut into 1- by 3-inch rectangles with a fluted pastry wheel. Make a 1½-inch lengthwise slit down the center of each rectangle. Push one end through slit and pull back. Let pieces rise for about 30 minutes.

Drop a few at a time into oil at 375°F. Fry until lightly browned on both sides. Remove with a slotted spoon and drain on paper towels.

Combine sugar and spices and sprinkle over Bugnes.

apple–crumb coffee cake

Yield: 1 8-inch-square coffee cake

1 recipe Sweet-Roll Dough
2 apples, peeled, cored, quartered, and sliced with the slicing disk
⅓ cup brown sugar
¼ cup all-purpose flour
1 teaspoon cinnamon
3 tablespoons cold butter, cut into 3 pieces

Prepare Sweet-Roll Dough as recipe directs. After kneading, pat dough into a greased 8 × 8 × 2-inch-square baking pan. Arrange apple slices over the dough.

Place the sugar, flour, cinnamon, and butter in the processor bowl and process with the metal blade until the mixture is crumbly, about 10 seconds. Sprinkle over apples. Let rise in a warm (80–85°F) place until doubled in bulk, 45 to 60 minutes.

Bake in a preheated 375°F oven for 35 to 40 minutes. Cool in pan 15 minutes. Remove to a rack. Serve warm.

scandinavian bear-track doughnuts

Yield: 24

1 package active dry yeast
½ cup lukewarm water (105–115°F)
¼ cup sugar
½ teaspoon anise seeds
¼ cup cold butter cut into 3 pieces
1 egg, room temperature
2½ cups all-purpose flour
Vegetable oil for deep-fat frying

Dissolve yeast in the lukewarm water in the processor bowl. Add sugar, anise, butter, egg, and 1¼ cups of the flour. Process with the metal blade for 15 seconds and let rise in the processor bowl for 20 to 30 minutes. Add remaining flour and process until a ball of dough forms on the blades, about 5 seconds.

Remove and knead for 1 to 2 minutes. Roll out dough to a 6 × 12-inch rectangle. Cut into 12 3 × 1-inch strips. Cover and let rise in a warm place (80–85°F) until doubled in bulk.

Slice the edges of each strip into "fingers" by making 4 cuts along the long edge of each strip, cutting through past the middle.

Deep-fry "tracks" in oil at 375°F a few at a time until a very light golden color. Drain on paper towels. Coat each with sugar by shaking in a paper bag containing sugar. Serve warm.

pizza dough with whole-wheat flour

Yield: 12 × 15-inch pizza or 12- to 14-inch round pizza

1 package active dry yeast
⅔ cup lukewarm water
(105–115° F)
2 teaspoons sugar
½ teaspoon salt
1 tablespoon vegetable or olive oil
1½ cups all-purpose flour
1 cup whole-wheat flour

Dissolve yeast in warm water in the processor bowl. Add sugar, salt, oil, and all of the all-purpose flour. Process with the metal blade for 15 seconds. Let rise for 30 minutes in the processor bowl. Add whole-wheat flour and process until a ball forms on the blades.

Remove dough and knead on a floured surface for 1 minute. Roll out into a large circle or rectangle to the desired thickness, about ⅛ to ¼ inch thick. Pinch up a rim around the edge.

Spread with the prepared Pizza Sauce mixture, shredded cheese, and desired toppings.

Bake in a preheated 400° F oven for 15 to 20 minutes, depending on thickness of crust. Cut into wedges and serve immediately with a cool beverage or wine and a tossed salad.

pizza dough with enriched flour

Substitute all-purpose flour for the whole-wheat flour.

pizza sauce and toppings

Yield: Sauce for 1 12- to 14-inch round pizza.

1 6-ounce can tomato paste
3 ounces (½ can) water
½ teaspoon garlic salt
2 teaspoons oregano
⅛ teaspoon freshly ground black
   pepper
1 to 2 tablespoons olive oil
4 ounces mozzarella cheese,
   shredded with shredding disk
2 tablespoons grated Parmesan
   cheese

Combine tomato paste with water and spread on prepared pizza dough. Sprinkle with seasonings and oil. Top with cheese and desired toppings.
Additional toppings may be added as desired:

Fresh mushrooms, chopped
   coarsely with metal blade or
   sliced with the slicing disk
Pitted black olives, sliced or
   chopped with the metal blade
Green peppers, chopped with the
   metal blade
Onion, chopped with the metal
   blade or sliced with the slicing
   disk
Pepperoni, sliced with the *serrated*
   slicing disk (What a joy it is to
   use the processor for this
   tedious task!)
Fresh parsley, chopped with the
   metal blade

Also:

Cooked ground beef
Cooked sausage
Anchovy fillets
Slivered ham
Fresh tomato slices or wedges

Picture on next pages: pizza with mushrooms, slivered ham, anchovies, and tomato slices served with a tossed salad and dry red wine

cookies

The food processor is a great pleasure to use for cookies, especially if an ingredient such as minced lemon peel or chopped fruit or nuts is required. The entire procedure — mixing, chopping, and blending — can be done in the food-processor bowl. Cleanup is done in a jiffy!

The metal blade is used to cream together the fat, sugar, and eggs. If an ingredient is to be finely chopped, it is added to this mixture and processed. Extra manipulation with the metal blade will do no harm to the fat mixture.

If an ingredient, such as nuts, is to be only coarsely chopped, it is added with the flour–baking-powder mixture. Here processing must be brief. If processed too much, the cookie becomes tough and the nuts minced.

which type of fat should be used in cookies — butter, margarine, or hydrogenated shortening?

These fats are not really interchangeable in cookie recipes. Butter and margarine contain 20 percent water and will cause cookies to spread too much and have thin, crispy edges when the recipe has been formulated for hydrogenated shortening. If the recipe specifies butter or margarine and hydrogenated shortening is used, the cookie will spread very little and be more tender and thick. For best flavor use butter in place of margarine unless the recipe calls for ingredients that would mask its flavor — molasses or strong spices, for instance. If you are trying to reduce dietary cholesterol, use margarine. It contains none.

what type of baking sheet produces the best cookies?

Use shiny baking sheets for cookies. Dark ones absorb heat and cause the cookies to burn on their bottoms before their tops are done. Shiny pans reflect oven heat and permit more uniform baking.

where in the oven should baking sheets be placed?

Cookies and other thin foods, such as biscuits, should be placed on the top oven shelf. This will prevent the cookie bottoms from burning before the tops are done. The middle and bottom oven racks are too close to the source of heat for even baking.

bourbon or rum balls

Yield: 4 dozen

> **5 dozen vanilla wafers, broken
>   (2½ cups crumbs)**
> **1 cup walnuts**
> **1 cup confectioner's sugar**
> **⅓ cup bourbon or rum**
> **3 tablespoons corn syrup**
> **Confectioner's sugar for coating**

Process vanilla wafers a few at a time with the metal blade until they are finely crushed. Remove to a mixing bowl and repeat until all are crushed.

Chop walnuts coarsely with the metal blade. Add to crushed wafers along with remaining ingredients. Mix well and form into 1-inch balls. Roll in confectioner's sugar and store in an airtight container for a week or two before using.

nurnberger lebkuchen

Spicy German cookies — so good!

Yield: 3 dozen

4 eggs
1⅓ cups sugar
⅓ cup candied fruit
½ cup almonds
1 teaspoon cinnamon
¼ teaspoon cloves
¼ teaspoon nutmeg
¼ teaspoon cardamon
½ teaspoon baking soda
2¼ cups sifted all-purpose flour

Place eggs and sugar in processor bowl and process with the metal blade for 1 minute. Add fruit, nuts, spices, and baking soda. Process 3 seconds. Add flour; process 5 seconds. Do not overprocess or the nuts and fruits will be pulverized. Refrigerate mixture 3 or 4 hours.

Spread mixture with a moistened knife into 1½ × 2½-inch bars, ¼ inch thick, on a well-greased and floured baking sheet. Let dry at room temperature overnight. Bake at 350°F for 20 minutes.

These will be hard at first and are best when served after storing for 2 weeks in covered containers.

russian tea cookies

Be sure to use *butter* in these. Margarine will not give the same flavor.

Yield: 3 to 4 dozen

1 cup cold butter, cut into 8 pieces
½ cup confectioner's sugar
1 teaspoon vanilla
½ teaspoon salt

2 cups sifted all-purpose flour
¾ cup walnuts
Confectioner's sugar for coating

Combine butter, sugar, vanilla, and salt in processor bowl. Process with metal blade until light, about 15 seconds. Add flour and process until a ball forms on the blades. Scatter the walnuts over the dough and process a few seconds or until nuts are distributed.

Remove dough and return one-quarter. Process until walnuts are coarsely chopped. Remove and repeat with remaining quarters.

Roll dough into 1-inch balls and place on an ungreased baking sheet. Bake at 400°F on the top oven shelf for 10 minutes, until set but not brown. Roll at once in confectioner's sugar. Cool on a wire rack and roll again in more sugar.

anise cookies

anise cookies

These licorice–lemon flavored cookies are usually served during the Christmas holiday season.

Yield: About 24

2 eggs	**¼ teaspoon salt**
Outer peel or rind of ⅓ lemon	**2 cups sifted all-purpose flour**
1 cup sugar	**½ teaspoon baking powder**
1½ tablespoons anise seeds	

Place eggs, rind, sugar, seeds, and salt in processor bowl. Process with the metal blade for 2 minutes.

Stir together the flour and baking powder. Add ½ cup at a time to the processor and process several seconds after each addition.

Remove and chill dough for at least 4 hours. Form into 1-inch balls and flatten to ¼ inch thick with a floured, chilled cookie stamp or the bottom of a patterned cut-crystal glass. Transfer to a greased and floured baking sheet. Cover with a paper towel and let dry at room temperature overnight.

Bake at 350° F for 15 minutes. Cool on a wire rack.

Picture on opposite page: nurnberger lebkuchen

apple–almond–rum bars

Yield: 20 bars, each about 2 inches square

- 2 eggs
- 1 cup sugar
- 2 tablespoons water
- 1 apple, peeled, cored, and cut into 6 pieces
- 1 teaspoon rum flavoring
- 2 teaspoons cinnamon
- ¼ teaspoon ground cloves
- ⅓ cup semisweet chocolate bits (optional)
- ¼ cup candied fruit
- 4 ounces almonds
- 2 cups sifted all-purpose flour
- 1 teaspoon baking powder

glaze

- 1 cup confectioner's sugar
- 1½ tablespoons water
- ½ teaspoon rum flavoring

Place eggs, sugar, and water in processor bowl. Process with the metal blade for 10 seconds. Add apple, flavoring, and spices; process 10 seconds. Add chocolate bits; process 5 seconds. Add fruit and almonds; process 5 seconds.

Stir together the flour and baking powder. Add to the mixture in the processor bowl and process just until blended, about 5 seconds.

Spread in a greased 9 × 13-inch baking pan. Bake at 350° F for 20 minutes.

Combine confectioner's sugar, water, and flavoring. Glaze bars while warm. Cool and cut into squares.

apple-almond-rum bars

zimtsterne (cinnamon stars)

zimtsterne (cinnamon stars)

These heavenly flavored, star-shaped cookies are served by my German relatives at Christmas. It used to be difficult for me to find ground almonds for this recipe. With a food processor, I make my own! Be sure to use an electric mixer to whip the egg whites. The food processor does not incorporate sufficient air into them.

Yield: 4 dozen

1 pound shelled almonds, blanched or unblanched	3 cups confectioner's sugar (stirred and spooned into the measuring cup)
4 egg whites	1 tablespoon lemon juice
¼ teaspoon salt	1½ tablespoons cinnamon

Process the almonds, half at a time, with the metal blade until they are finely ground, about 30 to 45 seconds.

Beat the egg whites with a mixer until soft peaks form; add salt, and gradually beat in the sugar. Set aside ½ cup of this mixture for a glaze. Stir the almonds, lemon juice, and cinnamon into the beaten egg whites and sugar mixture. Let stand for 20 to 30 minutes to allow almonds to soften.

Roll out small portions of the mixture to ¼ inch thick on a board sprinkled with confectioner's sugar. Cut into star shapes. (Or roll into walnut-sized balls and flatten.) Place on a greased and floured baking sheet and let dry at room temperature 3 to 4 hours.

Spread glaze on top of each. Bake at 300° F for 25 minutes. The glaze should remain light in color. Cool on a wire rack and store in an airtight container.

132

pies

pie crusts

The ideal pie crust is crisp, tender, flaky, and mild in flavor. Ordinarily these qualities are achieved by cutting hydrogenated shortening into a mixture of flour and salt, stirring in sufficient water to form a dough ball, and rolling out the dough.

During rolling, the flat pieces flatten and separate the moistened flour in layers. Steam formed from the water during baking separates these layers. The oven heat coagulates the protein (gluten) in the flour to form a crisp, flaky crust.

how small should the fat be cut?

If the fat is cut into large pieces, about the size of peas, the crust will have large flakes and be slightly tough. This is because the layers of dough between the flattened fat will be rather thick. If the fat pieces are extremely small, the crust will be quite tender and the flakes extremely small. For a crust that is both tender and flaky, fat particles about ⅛ inch in size are best.

how much water should be added?

If too much water is added or if the dough is mixed too long, the crust will be tough. Excess water and handling overdevelop the gluten (the protein) in flour. If too little water is added or if mixing is insufficient, the crust will be dry and crumbly. Flakes may not form because sufficient water is not available to form steam and separate dough into layers during baking.

what type of fat should be used?

Solid fats are best for forming a flaky crust because they can be cut into pieces; oils cannot. Butter and margarine are both 20 percent water and form a less tender crust than lard or hydrogenated shortening.

how can a soggy bottom crust be prevented in a fruit pie?

Several techniques may be used to prevent the juices from the filling from softening the bottom crust:

1) In fruit pies, use a minimum amount of sugar to sweeten the fruit. Sugar withdraws water from the fruit during baking; this water soaks through the crust.

2) Brush melted fat over the bottom crust before filling to "waterproof" it.

3) Place the pie initially in a very hot oven so the heat will cause the flour or starch or eggs used in the filling to thicken the filling quickly. Lower the heat to complete baking.

4) Use a little extra flour or starch in a fruit filling if the fruit seems to have a very high water content.

5) Never overbake custard pies. The network of coagulated egg shrinks, and the water separates out, soaking the crust.

what type of pie pan should be used?

Use a dull pan or a frosted aluminum pan. Shiny ones reflect the heat and the crust does not brown.

how can the food processor be used for preparing pie crusts?

Having made countless cardboard-like crusts while trying to discover a workable technique, I finally found one method that will not overwork the dough. Of course, the metal blade can be used in place of a pastry blender or two knives to cut the fat into the flour, but then another bowl and step are necessary to add the water.

The simplest procedure is to begin with very cold fat so it will cut cleanly with the blade. If too soft, the fat will not cut as well into uniform small pieces as it will when cut by hand. Embed pieces of cold fat, about the size of acorns, around and in the mixture of fat and flour in the processor bowl. Sprinkle all the water over the surface and turn the blades on and off quickly for 6 to 8 times or only until the fat is cut into ⅛-inch or slightly larger pieces.

If you cut in the fat and then use the machine to mix in the water, you will surely have an overprocessed, cardboard-tough crust without flakes. With the one-step method you'll have good results in one quick, easy step!

pastry for a double-crust pie

Yield: Crust for a 9-inch double-crust pie

2 cups sifted all-purpose flour
1 teaspoon salt
**⅔ cup plus 2 tablespoons very cold hydrogenated shortening, cut into 12
   pieces**
½ cup cold water

Insert cutting blade in processor bowl. Stir together the flour and salt and place in processor bowl. Arrange the shortening pieces around the bowl and embed them in the flour mixture. Sprinkle the water evenly over the surface. Process by turning the blades on and off quickly about 8 times.

Remove dough and form into a firm ball with the hands. Divide dough in half and roll out each on lightly floured waxed paper to 1 inch larger than the inverted pie pan. Ease one crust into pan; trim edge even with outer rim. Add filling; cover with remaining crust and fold edge under rim of bottom crust to make an edge 3 layers thick. Flute the edge. Cut a 1-inch hole in the center of top crust to allow steam to escape. Bake according to the filling directions.

alternate method

Shortening may be cut into the flour with the metal blade, turning it on and off quickly 8 times, until fat is cut into ⅛-inch pieces. Remove mixture to a bowl and add water gradually, pressing it into the flour with the tines of a fork until a ball of dough can be formed.

whole-wheat pie crust

Yield: 1 9-inch pie-crust shell

1 cup whole-wheat flour
¼ cup wheat germ
½ teaspoon salt
**½ cup cold hydrogenated
   shortening, cut into 6 pieces**
¼ cup cold water

Combine flour, wheat germ, and salt in processor bowl. Distribute fat and embed in mixture. Sprinkle evenly with water.

Proceed as directed in recipe for Pastry for a Single-Crust Pie.

pastry for a single-crust pie

Yield: 1 9-inch pie shell

1¼ cups sifted all-purpose flour
½ teaspoon salt
½ cup very cold hydrogenated shortening, cut into 8 pieces
3½ tablespoons cold water

Place metal blade in processor bowl. Stir together flour and salt and place in processor bowl. Arrange the shortening pieces around the bowl and embed them in the flour mixture. Sprinkle the water evenly over the surface. Process by turning the blade on and off quickly 6 or 7 times.

Remove dough and press into a firm ball. Roll out dough on floured waxed paper to 1½ inches larger than the inverted pie pan. Ease dough into pan without stretching. Trim crust ½ inch beyond the rim of the pan and fold edge under to make a double thickness of dough around the edge. Flute edge.

for a baked pie-crust shell

Prick bottom and sides with a fork. Place on the top shelf of a 450° F oven for 8 to 10 minutes.

for a crust to be baked with a filling

Do not prick bottoms and sides. Fill and bake as filling recipe directs.

alternate method

Shortening may be cut into the flour with the metal blade and water added gradually and mixed in with a fork (see recipe for Double-Crust Pie).

pâté brisée

I have used a tub margarine for this crust with great success. A favorite crust for Quiche.

Yield: 1 crust for a 10-inch quiche or a 9-inch single-crust pie

2 cups sifted all-purpose flour
¾ cup butter, cut into 6 pieces
1 large egg

Place flour in processor bowl. Embed butter in flour around bowl. Dribble egg over surface. Process with the metal blade for 8 seconds.

Gather the dough and form into a ball. Roll or pat out into an 11-inch circle on waxed paper. Invert into a 9-inch pie pan or a 10-inch quiche pan. Peel off paper. Pat evenly over bottom and up sides. Bake as selected filling recipe directs.

pâté brisée sucrée

Add ¼ cup sugar and 1 tablespoon lemon juice to recipe for Pâté Brisée. Use as a crust for fruit pies.

pretzel crust

Unique! Resembles finely chopped nuts in flavor and appearance.

Yield: 1 9-inch pie-crust shell

3 to 4 ounces pretzels, not too heavily salted, each broken into several pieces
⅓ cup cold butter, cut into 3 pieces (do not substitute margarine; flavor is not the same)
3 tablespoons sugar

Process pretzels with the metal blade until they are finely chopped. Measure out ¾ cup of the crumbs and return them to processor bowl. Add butter and sugar. Process until butter is finely cut in, about 20 seconds. A ball of dough does not form.

Press crumb mixture evenly on the bottom and up the sides of a 9-inch pie pan. Fill with a prepared filling. Crust softens if baked with an uncooked filling. This crust is delicious with chiffon or cream pies.

graham-cracker crust

Yield: 1 9-inch pie shell

24 graham crackers (to yield 1½ cups crumbs)
⅓ cup cold butter, cut into 5 pieces
¼ cup sugar

Process crackers with metal blade until fine crumbs form. Add sugar and butter. Process until well blended.

Press mixture evenly over the bottom and up the sides of a 9-inch pie pan. Chill or bake at 375° F for 8 minutes. Fill with a prepared filling.

cherry cream pie

This dessert always brings raves!

Yield: 1 9-inch pie

1 9-inch Pretzel Crust (see Index)
½ cup whipping cream, whipped
  with the plastic or metal blade
1 14-ounce can condensed milk
⅓ cup lemon juice
1 teaspoon vanilla
½ teaspoon almond extract
1 21-ounce can cherry pie filling

Prepare crust as recipe directs. Add the milk, lemon juice, and flavorings to the whipped cream in the processor bowl. Process just until blended, with the plastic or metal blade.

Pour at once into the prepared crust. Top with the cherry pie filling. Chill until firm. Garnish the edges with additional whipped cream before serving.

pumpkin pie

Yield: 1 9-inch pie

1 recipe Pastry for a Single-Crust
  Pie (see Index)
1½ cups Pumpkin Puree (see
  Index) or canned pumpkin
⅔ cup brown sugar
½ teaspoon salt
½ teaspoon ginger
¼ teaspoon cloves
½ teaspoon nutmeg
1½ teaspoons cinnamon
1½ cups milk (undiluted
  evaporated milk may be
  substituted for ½ cup milk)
3 eggs

Line a 9-inch pie pan with pastry.

Combine remaining ingredients in processor bowl and process with metal blade until blended. Pour into unbaked pie shell.

Bake at 400°F for 50 minutes or until a knife inserted 1 inch from the edge comes out clean. Center will be soft. Allow to cool for 20 to 30 minutes. Serve warm. Refrigerate remaining portion.

cranberry–pumpkin jewel pie

Bright cranberry chips rise to the surface of this pie.

Yield: 1 9-inch pie

To the recipe for Pumpkin Pie add ¾ cup cranberries to the filling mixture in the processor bowl. Process with metal blade 4 to 5 seconds, until cranberries are coarsely chopped. Pour into prepared shell and proceed as recipe directs.

apple pie

Yield: Filling for 1 9-inch pie

7 or 8 apples, peeled, cored, and quartered	2 tablespoons all-purpose flour
½ to ¾ cup sugar	1 teaspoon lemon juice
¼ teaspoon salt	Pastry for a Double-Crust Pie
1½ teaspoons cinnamon	2 tablespoons butter or margarine
	Egg white and sugar (optional)

Insert slicing blade in food processor. Place apples in tube, a few at a time, and slice, using firm pressure on the pusher. You should have about 5 cups of slices. Combine with salt, cinnamon, flour, and lemon juice.

Arrange in 9-inch pastry-lined pie pan; dot with butter. Place remaining pastry over apples; cut hole in top for steam to escape. Brush crust with egg white and sprinkle with sugar.

Bake at 425°F for 10 minutes. Turn oven down to 350°F and continue baking for 50 minutes.

speedy lemon–cheese pie

Yield: 1 9-inch pie

1 8-ounce package cream cheese, cut into 8 pieces
2 cups cold milk
1 package instant lemon pudding mix
1 9-inch pie shell (use baked Pastry for a Single-Crust Pie or one of the other crust recipes)

Place cream cheese, milk, and pudding mix in processor bowl. Process with metal blade until mixture is smooth.

Pour at once into a baked pie shell or prepared crumb crust. Chill until firm, about 1 hour. Top with fresh fruit, sliced with the metal blade, or canned cherry pie filling.

desserts

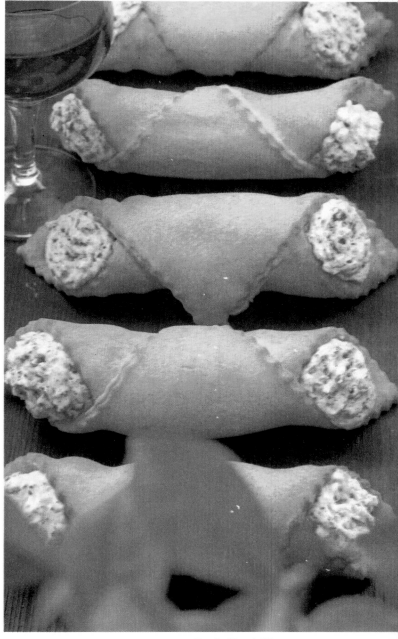

cannelloni alla siciliana

Yield: About 12

shells

> 2 tablespoons butter, melted
> 3 cups sifted all-purpose flour
> 3 tablespoons sugar
> ¼ teaspoon salt
> 1 egg
> ½ cup dry white wine

filling

> 1 pound ricotta cheese
> 1 cup confectioner's sugar
> ½ teaspoon vanilla
> ¼ cup candied fruit
> ¼ cup chocolate bits
> 1 egg white for sealing
> Vegetable oil for deep-fat frying
> Cannelloni molds or aluminum
> foil

cannelloni alla siciliana

Place ingredients for shells in the processor bowl and process with the metal blade until a ball forms on the blades. Remove and knead on a floured surface for 1 to 2 minutes. Cover, and refrigerate for 1 hour.

Place ingredients for filling in processor bowl and process with the metal blade until fruit and nuts are coarsely chopped. Refrigerate for 20 to 30 minutes.

Roll out dough on a floured surface to about ⅛ inch thick. Cut with a pastry cutter into 4- or 5-inch squares. Wrap each square diagonally (see photo) around a cannelloni form or a roll of aluminum foil. Seal corners with egg whites.

Deep-fry in oil at 375° F for about 3 minutes or until golden brown. Drain on paper towels and cool about 15 minutes with foil or forms still inside. Remove foil. Fill with cheese mixture and serve at once.

apple crisp

Yield: 4 servings

> 3 apples, peeled, cored, and cut
>   into quarters
> ½ cup brown sugar
> ½ cup whole-wheat flour
> ¼ cup cold butter or margarine,
>   cut into 4 pieces
> ½ teaspoon cinnamon
> ⅓ cup granola or quick-cooking
>   oats

Slice the apples with the metal slicing disk and toss with ½ of the brown sugar in a 1-quart casserole dish.

Place remaining sugar, flour, butter, cinnamon, and granola in processor bowl and process with the metal blade until crumbly. Sprinkle this mixture evenly over the apples. Bake in a 375°F oven for 30 to 40 minutes, until apples are tender. Serve warm.

cream puffs with fruit and whipped cream

Yield: 12

> 2 cups heavy whipping cream,
>   very cold
> ⅓ cup sugar
> 12 large Cream Puff Shells (see
>   Index)
> 1 small can mandarin oranges,
>   drained
> ¼ cup nuts, chopped with the
>   metal blade

Combine cream and sugar and whip until soft peaks form. (The metal blade does not whip air into cream well; use a mixer or whisk for greatest volume.)

Cut tops off cream puff shells and fill with the whipped-cream mixture. Garnish with mandarin oranges and chopped nuts. Serve immediately.

Picture on opposite page: cream puffs with fruit and whipped cream

cassata alla siciliana

When it's your turn to bring the dessert, bring this one. You'll be famous for it!

Yield: 8 to 10 servings

> 2 pounds ricotta cheese
> 1²⁄₃ cups sugar
> 1 teaspoon vanilla
> ¼ cup your favorite liqueur
> ¼ cup chocolate bits
> ¼ cup diced candied fruit
> 30 ladyfingers, halved lengthwise

Place cheese, sugar, vanilla, and liqueur in processor bowl. Process with metal blade until smooth and light, about 30 seconds. Add chocolate and fruit and process 2 or 3 seconds.

Line the sides and bottom of a 1½-quart casserole dish or springform pan with ladyfinger halves. Pour in one-third of the cheese mixture and cover with a layer of ladyfinger halves. Repeat two more times, ending with ladyfinger halves. Refrigerate overnight or for 4 to 6 hours. Carefully invert to remove from mold or remove sides from springform pan. Garnish with more candied fruit or cherries. Heavenly!

no-cook applesauce

Very good, so fresh-tasting!

Yield: 3 or 4 servings

> 4 apples, peeled, cored, and each
>   cut into quarters
> 3 to 4 tablespoons sugar
> 1 teaspoon lemon juice
> Dash cinnamon (optional)
> ¼ teaspoon antioxidant mixture
>   (optional if eaten quickly)
>   such as "Fruit Fresh" or
>   "ACM"

Place all ingredients in processor bowl and process with metal blade until smooth. Serve at once.

If apples are very large, process 2 or 3 initially and add remaining pieces through the tube as machine is running.

index